Coaching for Successful Solutions

www.coachmargie.com   Phone: 540.635.4843

# A Guide to Getting It:

# Remarkable Management Skills

Connie de Veer • Joyce Leonard
Margie Summerscales Heiler • Schuyler Morgan
Ursula Pottinga • Duane Reed • Chuck Schultz
Marilyn Schwader • Shariann Tom • John Vercelli
Mai Vu • Claire Walsh

Marilyn Schwader, Editor

CLARITY OF VISION PUBLISHING • PORTLAND, OREGON

Other books in the series:
A Guide to Getting It: Self-Esteem
A Guide to Getting It: Remarkable Management Skills
A Guide to Getting It: A Clear, Compelling Vision

For more information, visit www.ClarityOfVision.com
To order any of the *A Guide to Getting It* book series, visit www.AGuideToGettingIt.com

BOOK DESIGN AND PRODUCTION BY MARILYN SCHWADER

ISBN 0-9716712-2-2
Library of Congress Control Number: 2002112889
First edition: October 2002

# Table of Contents

# Acknowledgements

As the saying goes, "When the student is ready, the teacher will appear." I have been fortunate in my life to have had incredible mentors guiding me as I learn how to become a better leader. I thank them for helping me be a positive influence to those who have worked with and for me. In particular, I want to express my gratitude to the coaches who have contributed their knowledge and experience in the writing of this book. The student is still learning!

Marilyn Schwader, Editor

# A Note from the Editor

If you just picked this book up in the Business section of your local bookstore, you probably could have chosen any one of literally dozens of other books on the topic of management. What makes this book different is that the ideas and tools presented here come from the views of ten Business Coaches. Their perspectives provide reminders that when we approach the role of leader with openness, trust, and caring, we can be truly inspiring and remarkable managers.

This book is the third book in a series of books written by Life and Business Coaches that offer invaluable insights, examples, and exercises as guides to help the reader improve their business and personal life.

I invite you to read, explore, and enjoy!

Marilyn Schwader, Editor

# Enlarging the Lives of Others

## By Marilyn Schwader

My first management experience was at the tender age of seven, when I was asked by my second grade teacher to lead a group of my peers to create a paper-maché piñata for a party. Having never been placed in such a position, with little guidance from the teacher, and without any "learned" skills, I relied on my instincts to guide the others in my group. My teacher must have seen something in me that led her to believe I was capable of "managing" the project. The piñata was a success and my classmates were not only excited about the results, they came to look to me as a person who could lead. The project was a defining moment for me. I knew then that I wanted to be a leader, and much of my career has revolved around the management of others.

When I began to write this chapter, the idea of models of management swirled in my head. I pulled management books I had read from my bookshelves, and looked for that magic thought that would be something new for the reader and that might lead them to great success as a manager. After much thought, and some frustration with finding my "message," the realization hit me that perhaps we have all been looking for the holy grail of management in what "experts" say we *should* be doing. In fact, being a remarkable manager really requires that we get back to some basic truths about who we are and who we are leading. My being able to lead a group of seven-year-olds to accomplish a task without having any management school skills or models from which to operate indicates that we already have innate abilities that, when relied upon, can help us become remarkable managers. Although the topics presented in this chapter are not talked about in the business world to any great degree, they are fundamental to any relationship, and thus, lay a foundation that will allow you as a manager to develop yourself and your team in profound ways.

## The Greatest of These is Love

*"THE KIND OF LOVE WE SHOULD ADVOCATE IS THIS WIDER LOVE THAT YOU CAN HAVE EVEN FOR SOMEONE WHO HAS DONE HARM TO YOU: YOUR ENEMY."*

*~ THE 14TH DALAI LAMA OF TIBET*

You might wonder why a chapter on management skills would begin with a discussion of love. In every choice and every act, we as humans come from a place of either love (openness to possibilities) or fear. Unfortunately, business, with its competitive nature, is usually managed from a place of fear. We fear a loss of control, that someone else will make more money, that someone will have more power, that our ideas will be looked at as foolish. And so, many of us make our decisions, plan our objectives, and approach problem-solving based on what might *adversely* affect us, instead of looking at it from a perspective of possibilities—a place of love.

Coming from a place of openness requires the manager to look at the *why* instead of the *how*. The hoped-for result of the *how* is normal and essential. However, *why* we get those results is much more important. The *why* requires you to work more with ideas, beliefs, and relationships, all of which are impacted by whether you view them with a fear-based attitude or with love and openness. Beyond the typical management measurements of goals and financial ratios, it is necessary that managers embrace the idea of persons and what they bring to the organization in their ability, ingenuity, and talent. No business can amount to anything without the people who make it what it is.

In his book, *Leadership is an Art*, Max Depree tells the story of when his father, new to managing the furniture-making company Herman Miller, Inc., lost a key employee.

The millwright died, and not knowing what else to do, his father visited the bereaved family. While there, the widow asked him if it would be all right if she read some poetry. He agreed and she retrieved a bound book from another room and for several minutes read selected pieces of beautiful poetry. When she finished, his father commented on how beautiful the poetry was and asked who wrote it. She replied that her husband, the millwright, was the poet. What his father, and others since have wondered: Was he a poet who did millwright's work, or was he a millwright who wrote poetry?

What does this story teach us? To embrace the idea that we are all human, with "hidden" talents and skills. When employees are recognized for *all* of their abilities—not only in what they bring to their job, but what they contribute to the world outside the company—they will bring more to the work and service of the organization.

A remarkable manager liberates people to do what is required of them in the most effective and humane way possible. To do this, it is fundamental to have an understanding and acceptance of the diversity of people's gifts, talents, and skills. Accepting diversity allows us to think about the strengths of others, instead of trying to fit a person into a role, or trying to do everything on our own. Recognizing the gifts that people bring to work gives them an opportunity to give to the organization, and gives us as managers the chance to provide meaning, fulfillment, and purpose. A remarkable manager polishes and enables those unseen gifts that people have, making them shine. With love for that person and what they bring to their work, the *how* is taken care of and everyone is the better for it.

As businesses grow and staffs get bigger, managers know less and less about each employee. And in many cases, employees don't know much about each other. One company I worked for as a project manager ran into this problem when they grew from two employees to 50 in two offices, in addition to having several telecommuters. Although the company held regular gatherings to alleviate this problem, there were always those employees who couldn't attend. So, they found a way to solve the problem and celebrate the employees at the same time. They created a company yearbook. They had all employees fill out questionnaires asking about their favorite music, books, and movies, their ideal weekend, biggest challenge, and happiest childhood memory. Other fill-in-the-blanks included, "My role at..." and "What I really like about my job." The book devoted a full page, including a photo, to each person. Each employee received a copy and several copies were displayed in the company's lobby. The cost was minimal, but the benefits to both managers and the employees were enormous.

Another problem that exists for companies is the "Us vs. Them" dissension between managers and employees. When I was General Manager of an Apple computer retail store, my employees nicknamed me "Slash" because I made it a point to learn each of their jobs. When anyone asked them what I did, they would respond that my title was "inventory control, slash, administrative, slash, service, slash...." I learned the ins and outs of each area by having one-on-one contact with both the people working with the customers and with the customers themselves. The action opened communication, built trust, and because I knew all of the positions, allowed me to step in and help when necessary. My employees in turn began to feel comfortable finding ways to assist me in my tasks. The feeling at work changed from one of mistrust and low morale to that of helpfulness and pride in what we were doing. We also became a much more efficient team because ideas flowed. Employees felt safe sharing their input because I had made an attempt to understand their jobs. I not only stepped into their shoes, I took action, implementing changes from their suggestions and from what I saw wasn't working. Of course, this story would not have had nearly the type of ending it did, had I not been a fully active listener, one of the most important talents a manager can develop.

## Integrity is an Inside Job

*"A PERSON OF INTEGRITY IS ONE WHO HAS ESTABLISHED A SYSTEM OF VALUES AGAINST WHICH ALL OF LIFE IS JUDGED."*
*~ V. GILBERT BEERS*

Integrity is not so much what we do, as much as it is who we are. And who we are—our values—determine our actions. Values are like the sailor's sextant, guiding us through the latitudes and longitudes of life, providing us with internal measurements that we can rely on for resolving conflicting desires. All of us struggle with deciding between what we want to do and what we ought to do. Staying in integrity with our values determines how we respond, because those values determine who we are.

Socrates once said, "The first key to greatness is to be in reality what we appear to be." Remarkable managers remain consistent; they say and do the same thing. The more people see the level of integrity in a manager, the more trust there is. And establishing trust with others allows you to influence their lives.

Several years ago, I owned a restaurant in a college town. Most of my employees were high school and college students working part-time. One day a customer pulled me aside and asked if I might consider her daughter, Kay, for employment. She confided in me that Kay, a high-school junior, had been fired from her previous job because her boss had suspected her of stealing. She adamantly insisted that Kay had been in the wrong place at the wrong time and was innocent, but that the experience had left her daughter with low self-esteem and she had become discouraged in her subsequent job search due to the mark it had left on her job experience. Her mother asked if I would be willing to at least interview Kay and consider hiring her, even if it was just to wash dishes.

I had recently had some experience in overcoming false accusations in how I had handled what turned out to be a very public and traumatic end to a business partnership, and so had some understanding of her daughter's dilemma. Although my expectations weren't high, I agreed to interview Kay. What I encountered was a person with enormous potential who was carrying a great deal of mistrust and sadness due to her circumstances. I had significant empathy for her. I began by letting her know that her mother and I had discussed her situation. I then told her my own story of how people had wrongly perceived me, and that the biggest lesson I learned was to always ask for all sides of the story. Would she be willing to tell me her version of the events? She was surprised by my willingness to keep an open mind, and that I trusted telling her about my own situation. After a short hesitation, she explained in detail what had happened. Her story was plausible, and after she had answered all of my interview questions, I decided that she not only deserved another chance, but that she would probably be a very conscientious employee due to the experience. I emphasized to her that I was going against logic, that what seemed obvious I ought to do was not hire her, but that what I wanted to do was to give her a second chance. I told her that if I could trust her to be truthful and hardworking, she could have the job.

Kay worked for me for two years, as did her younger sister. They were two of the most dedicated, friendly, hardworking, and helpful employees I have ever worked with. Kay, who was extremely creative, continually gave me new ideas and was always willing to help when I was short-handed or needed a reliable person for a task. She eventually went to college, and we have kept in touch over the years. She regularly reminds me that if I hadn't been willing to trust her and give her an opportunity to rebuild her confidence, she might have made very different choices in her life.

By being in integrity with my values of staying open to the possibility that she was trustworthy, I was blessed with a tremendous employee, and I was able to influence a life in a most positive way.

## Serve Each Other

"REALLY BELIEVE IN YOUR HEART OF HEARTS THAT YOUR FUNDAMENTAL PURPOSE, THE REASON FOR BEING, IS TO ENLARGE THE LIVES OF OTHERS. YOUR LIFE WILL BE ENLARGED ALSO. AND ALL OF THE OTHER THINGS WE HAVE BEEN TAUGHT TO CONCENTRATE ON WILL TAKE CARE OF THEMSELVES."

~ PETE THIGPEN, EXECUTIVE RESERVES

When I was still in grade school, I heard a quote that altered forever the way I viewed my actions toward others. That quote was from Zig Ziglar, who said, "You can get everything in life that you want, if you help enough other people get what they want." As I incorporated Zig's concept into my actions, I started to look at every situation as an opportunity to find what I could do to help make other people's lives easier. I was not always successful, but by making an effort, I began to see the positive effect those actions had on other people, and ultimately for myself. My first inclination was to limit this to personal interactions. But, once I realized the value of this thinking, I soon applied it to all of my business interactions as well.

What would happen if each of us took the idea to heart and truly applied it to each interaction with others? Imagine how effortless our lives would become, and what we would have in our lives in return. If we were all looking out for and caring about how the other person would benefit, imagine how our work lives would improve.

The key is to do everything with no expectation of something returning. Then you will truly enjoy the effect on your life because it'll come back to you when you least expect it!

I'll give you an example of how this happened to me. One day at work, I had one of those days where it seemed everything was going backwards and upside down. My administrative assistant had not showed up for work, and I was deluged with phone calls from the corporate office and from customers. There was a sale in the store and we were short-handed due to the flu bug. My assistant finally arrived, looking harried and preoccupied. After giving her a few minutes to get settled in, and when I had a break in the action, I stopped by her office and stuck my head in her door. I asked if there was something going on that I might help her with. She explained that she had been dealing with a custody fight for her granddaughter and there had been some major developments that had left her emotionally drained. I realized that in comparison, my problems weren't that significant and decided to listen and give input if asked, but in the end did not mention how my day had been. By the end of the conversation, she had worked through much of her stress and sounded much calmer and somewhat relieved. She thanked me for listening to her situation and said she felt much better having talked to someone. My own problems with the day had also melted away during our talk.

The next day, I found a package on my desk from a customer. In it were both a compact disk of music and a thank you card with a quote by Woodrow Wilson: "You are not here merely to make a living. You are here in order to enable the world to live more amply, with greater vision, with a finer spirit of hope and achievement. You are here to enrich the world, and you impoverish yourself if you forget the errand." My "reward" had come to me in a totally unexpected way that was truly gratifying and uplifting.

One of the most profound ways that you as a manager can effect change is to come from a place of giving. Love is something you do for someone else; not something you do for yourself. When an action doesn't come naturally to you, it is an even greater expression of love.

To paraphrase Jacob Needleman, author of *A Little Book on Love*, all of us carry within us great possibilities, along with a great obligation. When we open ourselves to a life of consciousness that goes beyond our experience of happiness, knowledge, or meaning, we begin to understand what our lives are meant to serve. This consciousness allows us to see universal connections, and from that consciousness, the capacity to love.

Jesus said, in what many believe was his greatest sermon, "Give, and it will be given to you. A good measure, pressed down, shaken together and running over, will be poured into your lap. For with the measure you use, it will be measured to you." ~ Luke 6:38

Be like the ripples of water from a pebble dropped in a pond. Each person you touch, touches another, and outward unending. As Anne Frank said, "How wonderful it is that nobody need wait a single moment to improve the world." Start now. Smile, lend a hand, cheer someone on, talk to a team member about what's going on in his or her life. Thank those who are working for you for their efforts. Do it when least expected. Do it frequently. Do it with sincerity. Find out what someone really wants, and then help them get it.

## Do Unto Others

*"The hidden aspect of the 'great wisdom' is not so much a matter of which ideas are comprised by it, as it is the nature of the difficulty in putting these ideas into practice."*
*~ Jacob Needleman, A Little Book on Love*

I've written about some basic ideas that bring love, integrity, and service into the management picture. At the heart of all of my actions in the stories I have shared is a basic tenet that we all seem to know, but occasionally forget: "Do unto others as you would have them do unto you." You see, I desire compassion, learning, empathy, acceptance, and love from those I work with. How can I expect it from others if I'm not willing to offer it to them?

When you face a difficult decision that will affect an employee or your team, remember to put yourself in their shoes. Try on their position and feel what it might be like to be affected by that decision. Don't we all want to be loved, to have others act in integrity, and to be served? Do you ever remember a time when the person serving you was rude, or they ignored you? Have you ever had a boss who wouldn't share their reasoning with you? Do you ever get tired of someone saying they would do something, then not following through?

Have you ever done any of these things yourself?

People tend to criticize others most loudly in the area where they themselves have the deepest emotional need. Step out of your world and into the world of the person you are managing. Try to imagine the effect of your actions on those you work with.

In addition to the process of decision-making and making requests of your employees, the idea of "do unto others..." comes into play in the simple daily actions you take. The timely returning of phone calls, replying to requests, answering basic inquiries, and sharing information are all things that are impacted by this simple thought.

All human beings have distinct physical and psychological needs, and they're usually prepared to work to fulfill these needs. This is the basis of motivation and the key to productivity. By recognizing employees' needs you can create the conditions in which employees can work toward the fulfillment of those needs. Take care to remember that there is a big difference between making employees happy and keeping them from being unhappy.

How can you make your employees happy with their jobs? Using the "Do unto others..." approach, perhaps the most important way to impact an employee is to recognize them for their contributions. This is more than just giving them a pay raise. The focus is on the result, not the method. If someone does something in a different way, but still generates the desired outcome, give them a "pat on the back." Congratulate employees for their contributions in both ideas and the actual work done.

Another way to make employees happy is to make the work interesting and meaningful. An employee that seems bored with their work will be delighted to have the opportunity to do something different. Find ways to shake up their day in positive ways. Along the same thought process, find ways to provide enrichment opportunities. Give employees tasks that expand their learning and help them grow in their position and possibly into other areas.

A very important consideration in the "Do unto others…" category is to take care of minor grievances and gripes. Nothing destroys morale quicker and more effectively than neglecting irritants. Those irritants might not affect you directly, but ultimately they will impact your effectiveness as a manager. Remember to feel what it would be like as an employee to have to tolerate those annoyances. Then fix them.

## Remember the Little Things

*"To be really great in little things, to be truly noble and heroic in the insipid details of everyday life, is a virtue so rare as to be worthy of canonization."*

*~ Harriet Beecher Stowe*

This chapter has been written with the idea that we as managers can really do remarkable things by taking care of the basics, the "little things" that will influence in ways beyond our immediate experience. I ask you to maintain your delicate new way of managing from a place of love in a world crowded with cynics and skeptics. As in any process of change, you are bound to make some errors as you shed techniques that don't work and embrace the ideas I've presented.

As I write the ending to this chapter I'm struck by the irony that nothing that I've written about is "new thinking."

These concepts are as old as civilization. Take a step back, and you will move your organization forward. Learn again to stay open to all the possibilities with love in your heart, stay in integrity, serve others, and understand another person's feelings. Take care of the little things and you too, will become a Remarkable Manager enlarging the lives of others.

### References:

Chapman, Gary. *The Five Love Languages: How to Express Heartfelt Commitment to Your Mate*, Chicago: Northfield Publishing,1995.

DePree, Max. *Leadership is an Art.* New York: Dell Publishing, 1989.

Maxwell, John C. *Developing the Leader Within You.* Nashville, Tennessee: Thomas Nelson, Inc., 1993.

Needleman, Jacob. *A Little Book on Love.* New York: Doubleday, 1996.

## About
## Marilyn Schwader

As a Writing and Life Coach, Marilyn uses humor, compassion, and a strong sense of a writer's abilities to support and motivate her clients to become published authors. She has found that her purpose in life is to give a voice to subjects that benefit others. Her mission is to provide truthful, clear, and motivating information to those who passionately desire more in their lives. Her vision is to use her two passions—coaching and storytelling—to convey this information to as many people as possible.

Marilyn graduated from Oregon State University in Corvallis, Oregon with a Bachelor of Science degree in Technical Journalism with emphasis in Business Management. After working for several years as a technical writer contracting to high tech companies in the United States and Pacific Rim countries, she veered from the writing path and started her first business, M's Tea & Coffee House, in Corvallis.

Five years and numerous disastrous business mistakes later, she left the restaurant business and a short time later discovered coaching. In 1998 she enrolled in Coach University and started Clarity of Vision, a Business and Life Coaching practice. The law of attraction soon worked its magic, and her talents and experience in writing soon began drawing writing clients to her business.

During this time, Marilyn undertook a three-year project to compile and publish a book about her mother's family history. From that experience, she began helping people self-publish their books. Looking for a way to combine her coaching and writing experience, Marilyn decided to create a book series that would be written by coaches and that highlighted principles and ideas supported in the coaching process.

Thus, the *A Guide to Getting It* book series was born. *A Guide to Getting It: Self-Esteem* was published in January 2002. *A Guide to Getting It: Achieving Abundance* was published in August 2002. *A Guide to Getting It: Remarkable Management Skills* is the third book in the series.

For more information about Clarity of Vision Publishing, visit www.ClarityOfVision.com. To find out more about the *A Guide to Getting It* book series, visit www.AGuideToGettingIt.com. To contact Marilyn, send an email to Marilyn@ClarityOfVision.com or call 503-460-0014.

# Soft Skills Don't Have to Be Hard!

## By Connie de Veer

The American workforce is changing. Workplace demographics include more women, people of color, and diversely-abled professionals than ever before. The traditional values of a narrow focus, speed, efficiency, and a competitive spirit are being expanded to include a new paradigm that taps into the rich fund of ideas available from this expanding workforce. The search is also on by corporate visionaries and wise managers for ways to unite teams comprised of people from varying backgrounds and points of view. Creativity and inter-personal communication skills are emerging as vital to moving companies forward in the competitive market of the new millennium.

This new notion of the call to develop "soft skills" is buzzing around the corporate environment, creating a mix of responses that range from an enthusiastic, "Finally! What took you so long?" all the way to the caustic, "That has nothing to do with making widgets!" Arguably, most large organizations have all they can do to create whatever it is they are charged with producing for the consuming public. At first blush it *does* seem irrelevant to consider spending precious time and money on developing skills we like to think come naturally to us all, such as listening, creative thinking, and intuition.

But the fact is that these skills are proving to be sorely lacking within many corporations. High employee turnover is one result of a management culture that is not savvy with the soft skills that foster thinking "outside of the box," respect for individual working and learning styles, and commitment to a team-building philosophy that not only tolerates, but actually *celebrates and capitalizes on* diversity in all its manifestations.

Much of my work as a coach is centered around re-connecting individuals—managers and "managees"—with a way of thinking that is natural to the human experience, but unfortunately, seldom honored outside of the realms of childhood and artistic endeavors. Poet and corporate consultant David Whyte states in his book *The Heart Aroused: Poetry and the Preservation of the Soul in Corporate America*: "Yet the sound and the fury of an individual's creative life are the elemental waters missing from the dehydrated workday....Adaptability and native creativity on the part of the workforce come through the door only with their passions. Their passions come only with their souls. Their souls love the hidden springs boiling and welling at the center of existence more than they love the company."

I will pull from the language and experience I know best—that of the theatre, the actor's process in particular—to draw parallels between that lively art and the world of managing human beings within a large organization, with special emphasis on creative thinking and communication skills. Finally, it's not much different to galvanize a group of actors, designers, technicians, and writers toward the creation of a theatrical event, than it is to galvanize a group of equally talented and passionate professionals toward creating a product or offering a service based on a common corporate vision.

## Conjuring the "Hidden Springs"

There is a common misnomer that acting is about lying and good actors are good liars. Nothing could be further from the truth! The actor's process is, first and foremost, about awareness of self, and secondly about finding a point of connection with oneself and the experiences and characteristics of the character one is called upon to play. Openness, vulnerability, and empathy are the actor's tools of the trade. People go to the theatre to see their own myths and stories acted out upon the stage, and scrappy animals that we are, we can *smell* phoniness in an actor when we are sitting in the audience. We know when the actor has put on the mask of character to cover up, and when she is using the character's mask to *reveal* universal elements of the human condition we all share. Our "souls love the hidden springs boiling and welling at the center of existence," as Whyte states, and it is this experience of authenticity and vulnerability that moves us and has kept the theatre alive all these centuries.

So what place does this boiling and welling passion have inside the sturdy, business-like walls of the corporation? Well first of all, whether we like to admit it or not, it's there already! Passion, soul, emotion, and all things soft and murky are part and parcel of the human animal and try though you might, you can't get rid of them. But there are ways to call forth the richness of passion and creative energy and channel it into a workforce far more productive and dedicated than you ever could have done by fearing it or seeking to control and stifle it.

### Exercises and Inquiries

1. **What Role will you play?** Conjure up an image of a real or imagined person/character/archetype whose qualities you would like to evoke in your managerial role overall, or on a particular project. For example:

   - I will be Apollo, fearlessly steering the chariot of fire into a new day!
   - I will be like the Unsinkable Molly Brown, refusing to let my team give in to discouragement. I will hold them big and call forth their instincts to thrive, using humor and high energy.

2. **Being vulnerable and speaking the truth.** Consider the following inquiries. To deepen your learning, you may also wish to journal and meditate on them as well.

   - What am I protecting?

- How does that serve me? My staff?
- How does it undermine my efforts? And my staff?
- Where am I not telling the truth?
- What's it costing me? How is it impacting my staff?

## Holding Powerful Space: Belief, Intention, and Allowing

The theatre originated as a sacred ritual space where tribal members gathered to muse about the meaning of existence, evoke a Sacred Presence, and tell stories. The theatre borrows that notion of sacred space as the blank canvas upon which anything may be created. The act of group creation depends upon the dynamic of *community,* with trust and inclusion as its keystones.

But how do we make the jump from the comfort and mystery of a primitive ritual gathering around a fire to the corporate boardroom? Mystery and the necessarily messy process of creativity do not readily leap to mind as highly valued components of contemporary western corporate culture! In her book *Leadership and the New Science: Discovering Order in a Chaotic World*, Margaret J. Wheatley draws a distinction between *control* and *order.* "If we believe that there is no order to human activity except that imposed by the leader, that there is no self-regulation except that dictated by policies, if we believe that responsible leaders must have their hands into everything, controlling every decision, person, and moment, then we cannot hope for anything except what we already have—a treadmill of frantic efforts that end up destroying our individual and collective vitality." Wheatley asserts, and I agree, that there is a natural order in nature and all living things. There is a "self-organizing" thrust to life itself. However, on the surface it may appear chaotic. Skillful managers trust this phenomenon. The primary means they have of achieving this is acknowledgement of the concept of *space*.

For anything to be created there must be space. My training from The Coaches Training Institute offers the concept of "holding the space" for clients as a bedrock component of the co-active coaching model. What do we mean by this? It has to do with how one regards another, what **beliefs, attitudes, and expectations** we hold about that person. I learned early in my work as a university professor that a student's ability to perform had a direct correlation to whether I believed they could or not—further testament to the awesome responsibility of leadership.

Let's face it, human beings are animals—and like it or not, predatory ones at that! And as such, we are hard-wired to sense danger in any space. In emotional, psychological realms—where most of us feel particularly vulnerable and at risk—our sensors are programmed to "smell" any potential threat to our existence, our very identity itself. People know, perhaps only at the unconscious level, but they *know* when they are not being seen and regarded as fully as they know themselves to be. And this limited regard and expectation of professionals by those in positions of leadership profoundly impacts their ability to perform. And the ultimate manifestation of holding people "small," as we say in "coachspeak," is a decline in corporate productivity and profit, not to mention the toll in human dignity and the loss of vast stores of creative wisdom.

Another step in holding the space is **setting an intention**. I'm not referring to planning the items on a meeting agenda, but rather to giving deep consideration as to *how* as well as what you desire to accomplish in a group. For example, what qualities do you want to infuse the space with? How will you *be* in order to elicit creative interaction and free, yet mutually respectful self-expression in your next group gathering?

A large component of holding powerful space has to do with the fine art of **allowing.** Honest introspection on this issue can yield potent results. Exercise #4 that follows can be a useful tool in your mindful creation of a management style that balances healthy boundaries and expectations such as deadlines and corporate policies, with an attitude of trust in the inherent resourcefulness and creativity of your team members.

### Exercises and Inquiries

1.  To help clarify your intention in your own mind, before your next meeting, **create a metaphor** to describe how you feel about a meeting or meetings you have led in the past. This will not be something you need to share with your team members unless you feel it necessary. It will serve to align your own state of being with your conscious intention(s) for the group dynamic. For example:

    *   I feel like I'm leading a climb up Mount Everest and everyone's lives are in *my hands*!

    *   I'm the head surgeon performing brain surgery on the U.S. President. Everyone's *got* to concentrate, be quiet, and make no mistakes!

    *   I am a six-year-old trying to get a group of grumpy parents to go along with my party idea.

2.  Design a metaphor to describe the kind of space *you wish to create*. For example:

    *   King Arthur's Roundtable – Everyone present will be noble and brave, equally responsible for creating policies.

    *   A Giant Playroom – where we all express ourselves freely and in the moment. It's lively, colorful, and full of fun and laughter.

    *   A flock of geese, taking turns at leading the v-shaped migration back to our home.

3. What will you fill the space with? Explore this question both literally and metaphorically. For example:
   - I will charge the room with excitement, like a bolt of lightning!
   - I will fill the space with lots of permission for my team to share all their ideas without judgment.
   - I will hold enormous space in the room and raise the bar for my team members.

4. In your own private journaling and contemplation time, consider the following questions:
   - Where am I too tight on the reins (therefore stifling a member or members of my team from coming forth with their full commitment and creative contribution)?
   - Where am I too loose on the reins (for example, what am I tolerating that is undermining the overall structure and support of the team's functioning as a whole)?
   - What's another metaphor I want to create for my own management style regarding the art of allowing—other than the perceived need to "rein people in"—that will really hold them big?

## Trust: The Touchstone of Team-building

Rest assured that precious few people have access to motivation or commitment to the company mission, let alone venture forth with a new idea or creative suggestion, without an environment of trust. If you are hoping to facilitate a team toward achieving their highest potential as a group, foster trust in them as individuals first.

Get really clear about what the **boundaries** are. What are your expectations regarding time management, for example? Is it acceptable for your team members to come and go from the workplace, as long as they get their work done? Or is it necessary for them to be present in the workplace according to specific hours? Why? Have you made that absolutely clear to them? Has management changed recently? If so, have you made an effort to learn the rules of the game set forth by your predecessor and have you clearly communicated your own changes?

Boundaries differ from constraints in that they are created for the intention of providing safety and integrity in the workplace. People feel empowered and respected as the adult professionals they are when everyone is "on the same page," as we say.

### Exercises and Inquiries

I.  Sacred Space

This exercise is suitable for a retreat due to its obvious time requirements and sensitive nature. The physical make-up of the room is an important element in creating sacred, safe space for people to share their inner most selves with each other. I suggest chairs in a circle to create a sense of equality and community. (Think like a theatre set designer or stage director and consider how you want the participants to feel in the space, what your role is, and what your metaphor is for how you want to hold the space.)

As a manager and facilitator, being an equal participant in this exercise is vital. You will answer the questions like everyone else. Likewise, invite everyone to participate as fully as they feel comfortable. The point of this exercise is to share deep parts of oneself with the group and to have the group hold big, trusting, open space for one another *and to carry that degree of trust forward into the work environment*. If someone does not participate, yet still remains present in the room, they are in effect saying, "I do not and will not trust you." That is of course, detrimental to the entire group.

**One hard and fast rule to this exercise is confidentiality.** Be absolutely clear with the group that nothing will leave the room following the exercise. Trust must be earned and honored on an ongoing basis, otherwise it's not trust!

Ask the following questions and make clear to the group that trust will build if everyone agrees to consider each question deeply and answer honestly. **Rule number two** is that emotional responses be allowed, but that group members simply listen and not jump in and try to fix or even talk about the issue. Just listen and learn as you go around the circle allowing each member to answer the questions.

1. Who has influenced your life the most?
2. What is the most perfect thing in nature?
3. When in your life did you feel the most loved?
4. What's your biggest fear?
5. What do you think is the most essential part of your true self?
6. When did you feel the most alone?
7. If you were an animal (other than human), what would you be?
8. What do you find most in need of change in the world?
9. What's the worst boundary one can violate in another?
10. What does freedom feel like to you?
11. What part of the world fascinates you the most?
12. What part of yourself do you try not to let others see?
13. What brings you the most joy?
14. What's the loneliest part of the day for you?

15. What was your favorite room in the house you spent time in as a child?

16. If you could choose one day of your life to live over again, what would it be?

17. What makes you the angriest?

18. What do you love the most?

19. What is the most moving music you've ever heard?

20. What do you want to be remembered for after you die?

## The Fool's Wisdom: Fanning the Creative Fire

"LIFE IS THE GAME THAT MUST BE PLAYED."
~ E. A. ROBINSON

Shakespeare uses the role of the fool in his plays as the wisest character in the play, and the one who speaks the truth, albeit in riddles. This archetype is a powerful combination of playfulness and wisdom—qualities we tend not to think of as partners. But studies have shown that play is a skill that mammals must learn in order to survive. Doesn't that just blow the lid off our Puritanical notion of play as a frivolous, unnecessary indulgence? Further studies reveal that motor development and emotional growth peak at the same time in child development *only if and when the child has been allowed ample opportunities for free play and exploration.* Play hard-wires core survival tools into the brains of mammals, yielding the tool of creative problem-solving as a means of avoiding danger, as well as evolving the species.

I hear the phrase "creative thinking" bandied about in the workplace, and I see earnest attempts being made to recognize the need to grow and further utilize this skill to facilitate corporate productivity and workplace morale. But often such attempts are not as successful as they could be because the vital spirit, or attitude of playfulness, is absent. Corporations are under the gun of time constraints; but unfortunately, that, combined with the expectation placed on employees to improve performance in a measurable way, dampens the spirit of play. What to do?

The following exercises, again more suitable for a retreat setting away from the work environment, are designed to foster a playful atmosphere and from that perspective, develop creative thinking skills.

### Exercises

I. "My Bonnie"

This exercise will (hopefully) squeeze out the stodgy grown-up in everyone and get him or her to connect as a group without feeling called upon to "perform." It's a great warm-up and ice-breaker that the creative folks at Chicago's improvisational club *Comedy Sportz* use to get their audiences ready to play.

Everyone stands in front of a chair. The group sings the familiar song:

> "My Bonnie lies over the ocean,
> My Bonnie lies over the sea,
> My Bonnie lies over the ocean,
> Oh, bring back my Bonnie to me.
> Bring back, bring back,
> oh bring back my Bonnie to me, to me!
> Bring back, bring back,
> oh bring back my Bonnie to me, to me!"

Simple enough, no? Now…have everyone begin sitting in their chair, but they must stand up whenever they say a word in the song beginning with the letter "B."

Have fun!

II. Go/Stop/Fall

This is another good ice-breaker, with the added benefits of unlocking the creative fount available in the body, and building camaraderie.

- GO - Begin by having the group simply walk around the room. (Pay attention to how they do this, too. It will reveal much about the existing team dynamic as well as these particular individuals. Be mindful about regarding them with curiosity and respect, NOT judgment. Are they all moving in a clockwise direction? How close do they get to each other? Are they making eye contact?)
- STOP – When you say "stop," they're to freeze in whatever position they're in.
- FALL – When you say "fall," they're to fall IN SLOW MOTION to the ground. (This is to avoid injury! If you have diversely-abled people in your group, let them find a creative way to "fall" that they're capable of doing.)
- Have them GO or STOP or FALL with the following circumstances: (Have fun and make up your own, too!)
    1. In a room filled with helium.
    2. In a giant vat of bread dough.
    3. Like a slow motion version of a Jackie Chan flick.
    4. Like you're starring in a shampoo commercial
    5. Like an FBI agent.
    6. In a bubble gum factory that is overflowing with bubble gum.
    7. On a playground covered in olive oil.
    8. Like the stars on "Bay Watch."

III. Get Out of The Box!

This exercise was inspired by Roger von Oech's book *A Whack on the Side of the Head: How You Can Be More Creative.* von Oech asserts that the creative process requires that four basic roles be present for an idea or project to reach fruition. These roles may be realized in one person working solo, or assumed by members of a team on a group project. The roles and their functions are:

1. The Explorer – responsible for exploring new ideas, daring to venture forth into dark, untrod territory, searching, and researching for clues, details, and valuable nuggets.

2. The Artist – looks at things from all angles, looks for new ways of organizing or conceiving of things, imagines possibilities, plays, and sometimes even breaks the rules!

3. The Judge – discerns whether the idea is valid, what the outcomes may or may not be, anticipates potential problems, analyzes data, and is not afraid to make a decision.

4. The Warrior – makes it all happen with courage, tenacity, strategic thinking, energy, and drive.

Divide team members into small groups, if necessary. Have them take turns playing each of the four roles described above, while they attempt to solve the following problems. Ideally, have a box of silly props, hats, and costume pieces that they can use. It's also liberating and inspiring to play silly music, like Rossini's *William Tell Overture* (you know, the Lone Ranger theme).

- They must remove their naked (please...have them use their imaginations for this "costume!") 104 year-old grandfather from a burning building, but he's barricaded himself in with mounds of jello.

- They are performing a delicate surgical operation with medical students and high-powered doctors filling the viewing gallery. The head surgeon is drunk.

- They are stranded on a life raft in the middle of the ocean. They can see an island off in the distance. But there are sharks swimming around the raft. They must decide what to do and then implement it.

## "In Form and Moving..."

Hamlet extols the human body with the words:

"What a piece of work is man! How noble in reason! How infinite in faculty! In form and moving how express and admirable!"

Yet the belief our culture tends to labor under is more reminiscent of the melancholy Dane a few scenes earlier when he opines:

"O, that this too, too solid flesh would melt
Thaw and resolve itself into a dew!"

Thus our feelings toward our bodies are equally ambivalent. If you're feeling uneasy or judgmental regarding the relevancy of the subject of movement and the body in a book about Management, you come by it honestly! As a culture, we at best try to avoid the body by "clinicalizing" it (calling it "it," for example, as if it were a separate thing not really a part of us), regarding it as just something necessary for our survival, something to be controlled, conquered, or ignored altogether. And at worst, we exploit the body through degrading perversions and extreme indulgences. Both of these separate us from our bodies. One result of that is the loss of a healthy respect for the body's inherent wisdom, incredible facility for learning and adaptability, resourcefulness as a gauge for sensing emotion, and through its own brilliant language, the ability to provide us with insights, intuition, and creative ideas.

The following exercises are designed to re-connect participants with their bodies as an integral part of the Self, and to learn (most likely re-learn what we knew as children), how to access the body's unique wisdom. They are designed to at once relax and vitalize the self by releasing excess muscle tension, increase oxygen and bloodflow to the brain, awaken the senses, and calm the mind. What could be accomplished if everyone showed up for work in that state of being!

Exercises

I. Centering

This is an excellent way to focus the mind and set a positive intention for the day, or for preparing to give a speech or presentation. If you have studied martial arts you may recognize some similarities.

- Stand or sit comfortably and without trying to change anything, simply notice what your body is feeling, sensing, doing.
- What's your breathing like? Is your jaw tight? Can you feel your heart beating? Are you holding excess tension anywhere?
- Place a hand on your abdomen and release those muscles and any others you might be tensing excessively.
- Gently concentrate on letting your inhalation reach all the way down to those muscles.
- Breathe like this for at least one minute.
- Now imagine warm light beginning to glow at the center of your body where your hand rests.
- Imagine that light radiating from your center to all parts of your body, healing, energizing, and reinvigorating.
- Now imagine the light radiating beyond your body in 360 degrees.
- Create an intention for what you want to send out into the world and imagine this radiating light carrying your intention from your center into the world.
- Open your eyes. How do you feel? What do you notice?

II. Whole body listening
- Have the group divide into pairs by counting off "1, 2."
- Each person will tell their partner a story about an event they experienced that was highly emotional for them. **They will have five minutes to tell their story.** (You'll have to remember to bring a timer to the retreat!)
- The listening partner will concentrate on listening to the story with their whole body. Instruct them to pay close attention to:
  — the words of the story.
  — the storyteller's tone and quality of voice.
  — the storyteller's body language and movement.
  — their own body's responses to the story (for example, increased heart rate, sensations of empathy manifested physically, like "I feel like there's a rock in my stomach").
- The listener will then share what they "heard" with their partner **for five minutes.**
- Have the partners switch roles and repeat the exercise.

## Questions to Process and De-brief

Lock in the learning with team members by holding big space for them to process the events of the retreat. Be prepared for emotional responses you may not see in each other on a daily basis at work. Affirm for your team that their showing up today and sharing their deepest, most vulnerable selves is an honor for everyone present. Congratulations! You have all created sacred space.

1. What did you learn?
2. Where did you stop short?
3. What got in the way of your fully committing?
4. Does this obstacle show up in your life in other ways?

5. What did you learn about yourself?
6. What did you learn about the group?
7. Who in the group "showed up" in the biggest, most courageous way?
8. What is the voice in your head saying when you get stuck?
9. What will you choose to replace that voice with?
10. How will you integrate today's learning into your work?
11. What new, wild, and crazy idea will you try out this week?

### A Final Word

The time is now ripe for savvy managers to stretch themselves and their team members into the rich and vast resources of the human creative spirit. Claiming ownership of our power to create is the most salient element to be gleaned from the art of the Theatre. Great civilizations through the ages are measured first and foremost by the art and philosophy they produce, then by scientific discovery, and *finally* by commerce. Creative endeavors convey the beliefs, degree of sophistication, influence on other cultures, and inner spirit of a people. Cultures throughout history that are noted for making the most significant contributions to the evolution of the planet are cultures that fostered creative self-expression and independent thinking.

Everyone benefits from a creative culture. Combine the power of community derived from the necessity for team creation inherent in the Theatre, with a mission of employer-employee co-creation, and you have a recipe for success in an expanding and evolving workplace. To quote Hamlet yet again, "The play's the thing!"

## About
## Connie de Veer

After 15 years of teaching Acting, Connie de Veer, CPCC, made the transition from a tenured associate-professorship at Illinois State University to full-time coaching. She holds a Master of Fine Arts degree from The University of Texas at Austin. Prior to her academic career, she was a professional actor, singer, and dancer, and a member of Actor's Equity Association. She received her coaching training and certification from The Coaches Training Institute in San Rafael, California. She is the 2002 Chapter Leader for the Bloomington/Normal Chapter of the International Coach Federation. She is also a certified teacher of the Alexander Technique, a system for developing self-awareness and re-educating habits of physical movement and overall use of the self. She received her training at The Urbana Center for the Alexander Technique.

Connie divides her practice between coaching and teaching private lessons in the Alexander Technique. She is also an authorized distributor for Inscape Publishing, creator of leading edge assessments and learning resources.

Connie has created *The Comprehensive Stress Management Program*, which combines coaching, the Alexander Technique, the Coping & Stress Profile® from Inscape Publishing, and a twelve week curriculum of assignments and self-awareness exercises designed to empower participants to change their negative responses to stressful stimuli by changing their beliefs, movement patterns, and behavior choices.

Connie's experience as a master teacher, director, and choreographer equip her with the means to inspire her clients to develop their creativity, intuition, emotional intelligence, and communication skills. Her coaching encourages clients to acknowledge their bodies as a valuable instrument for self-awareness and expression. She believes passionately in the power of play and physical movement to unlock "stuck" thinking and release authenticity.

You can reach Connie at 309-827-3350, or at CdVcoaching1@aol.com, or visit www.cdvcoaching.com.

# The Art of Saying "No"

---

## By Joyce Leonard

*"In order for things to change, you must change. In order for things to be different, you must be different."*
~ Unknown Author

Throughout your career, you have been encouraged to answer with a resounding "YES":

"Yes, I'll cancel my personal appointment and work late again tonight."

"Yes, I'll skip lunch so we can discuss that new assignment."

"Yes, I can overlap and attend two meetings at once."

"Yes, I'll be a tougher person at work so my employees will respect me."

Again and again, you give pieces of yourself away, leaving little time to get your own work done and to enjoy your life. In the short run, you're crazy-busy, existing on adrenaline, caffeine, and sugar to keep you going; in the long run you become paralyzed, dispassionate, disillusioned—in other words, burned out.

Since your employer will never send you to a class on how to say "No," you will need to learn this secret skill on your own. The following pages will provide you with practical tips from those in the trenches—the courageous people who took the chance and said "No" and found, to their amazement, that the sky did not come crashing in on them! In this chapter, you will find out how to take your life back and be more productive on the job—how to say:

- "No" and keep your personal time.
- "No" to a packed schedule with little time to work *on* the business.
- "No" to attending every meeting that you're asked to join.

- "No" to becoming tougher in order to be a more "effective" manager.

Join the growing group of managers who have done this and are now experiencing an incredible feeling of freedom and control on the job that they never thought possible!

## Say "No" and Keep Your Personal Time

My very first experience with saying "No" at work was several years ago. I had to leave work one day precisely at 5:00 to be on time for a personal appointment. I was practically out of my cube, purse in hand, when my phone rang. I froze in my tracks for a few seconds, not knowing what to do. This call could possibly take several minutes and I didn't have any time to spare. I struggled with not answering—we are so committed to putting work before our personal lives. How could I *not* answer that phone? Well, I decided then and there, that my commitment to my appointment was top priority, and I let that phone call go to voice mail. And do you know what happened? The world did not come to an end—the person left a voice mail, and it wasn't urgent. I picked it up the next morning. Nothing *bad* happened. In fact, for the first time that I could remember, I had put myself first and let work wait until the next day.

When I tell this story at my *"Say No"* workshops, I see the fear and disbelief in the faces of many participants. "What if it was the boss?" someone asks. "What if someone needed something that night?" asks another. The truth is this: if it's an emergency, you can be paged and then you can discuss the options at that time. In my experience, and from the success stories of those who have attended my workshops, most telephone calls are not emergencies. If you put your life on hold so that you'll be available to answer every call— every need—your life will never begin. If you've got some place to go, let the calls go to voice mail.

Putting ourselves first is often thought of as a luxury— something we put off until all our tasks are done and no one wants any more from us. We get into the mindset that when we're tired, we need to push harder, when in fact, that's the time to take a break. Breaks are a time to regenerate. By taking just ten minutes to think about something other than work, you will come back refreshed and more creative than you were before. Some people walk outdoors, others read poetry, look at a beautiful picture, listen to their favorite music, or call a good friend. I walk down to my car and listen to a ten-minute relaxation tape. When my break is over, I am so rejuvenated that it feels as if I've been off work for several hours! Whatever you do, have it be something that gives you joy—don't read the front page of the newspaper with its constant barrage of bad news.

A magazine article a few years back highlighted what high-level executives did to reduce stress. All of them said that they regularly scheduled time out for themselves—time spent not thinking about work, but doing something that they truly enjoyed. The idea of taking a break is analogous to the philosophy of the airlines: in case of an emergency, put the oxygen mask on yourself first, then assist others. It's also the philosophy of financial planners: pay yourself first. If we don't put ourselves first by taking care of ourselves first, we won't have anything to give to others, to our work, or to our passions. If we spread ourselves too thin, we won't even be there anymore. Having and keeping your personal time is not a luxury anymore—it's survival!

***Take Action:*** Take a moment right now to think about how you can incorporate more personal time into your day. Is it blocking out break time on your schedule? Will you keep your personal appointments and let the calls go to voice mail? What other ways can you get pieces of your life back? Commit to saying "No" *one time* this week in order to keep your personal time. Doing this will feel awkward at first, but you will soon see that it is actually very easy—because nothing bad happens!

## Say "No" to a Packed Schedule and Have Time to Work on the Business

There is a difference between working *in* the business (or in the job) and *on* the business. Working in the business consists of activities such as attending meetings, processing voice mails and emails, meeting with clients, working with employees, and completing tasks. Working *on* the business is when you devote time to create—because you can't create if you're always doing. When you stop what you're doing and spend time to create, you can think strategically, see the bigger picture, gain a different perspective, and then create strategies and tactics to be more organized, productive, effective, profitable, and a better manager.

I was told of a CEO who found his creative time so useful that he now has an entire department assign a specific time to create. From 10:30 – 11:30 every morning there are no phone calls, emails, voice mails, meetings, or pages. No one can interrupt anyone in that department during that time. What he started seems impossible to imagine in the beginning, but it is now the norm. Workers there say it is so quiet, you can hear a pin drop. Everyone respects that time for focusing on the business—business plans, strategies, action plans, and the like are created and worked on during this time every day. In that department, business results increased dramatically.

Time to think and plan—can you imagine one hour every day with no interruptions? What would that do for the business and for you? One of my clients decided to take me up on this concept. In her office, everyone is connected to the same on-line calendar and can schedule meetings for anyone in the group. At the beginning of the month, she blocked off every day from 11:30 – 1:00. Not only was she going to dedicate one hour a day to create, but, doggone it, she deserved a half hour lunch everyday as well. Within a week, the inevitable call came in from a teammate,

"Everyone's available for a meeting next Tuesday from 12:30 – 1:30 except you, can you move whatever you've got at that time for us?" The moment of truth had arrived—what should she do? Should she admit that the time was "only" there for her to work on the business? Fortunately, she had already experienced the increase in creativity, focus, and productivity that working *on* the business provided her, so she took a big gulp and asked some questions. She found out what was on the agenda, what part she played, and then together she and her teammate worked out a win/win solution: the agenda would be shifted around so that she could join the meeting right at 1:00. She held on to her time and was able to be there for her teammates. Taking this approach was not easy or natural for my client; her tendency is to put everything aside for others. However, in making a commitment to her own success, she got creative and everyone ended up getting what they needed. As it turned out, she spent part of her hour working on the meeting she was going to attend, making it much more productive. Realizing that preserving time on her schedule to work on the business made her more focused, more creative, and allowed her to get more things accomplished, she was able to let go of the guilt of not being at her coworkers' beck and call. What was at first considered a luxury—working on the business—was now a necessity. Saying "No" was crucial to her survival!

**Take Action:** Look at your schedule for a moment. How busy is it? Have you dedicated any time to work *on* the business—to create, organize, and plan? How would you feel at the end of the week having taken the time to do this? Take a minute right now to block out time on your calendar to work on your business. Commit to saying "No" *one time* this week in order to keep that time. You will feel guilty at first, but you'll soon see that you are more focused, more creative, and get more things accomplished!

A word about packed schedules and back-to-back meetings. Packed schedules and back-to-back meetings actually cause you to be defocused and waste your time and energy. Here's how: it's 15 minutes before the hour and the meeting you're in looks like it might not wrap up right on the hour. Your next meeting is on the hour, leaving you no time to physically and mentally transition, nor to use the restroom. Now, for the next 15 minutes, you're not focusing on your current meeting. Instead, you're wasting energy fretting about whether you should leave this meeting early, be late to the next, and worrying that you'll not have time to go the bathroom ("Oh, I'll just hold it for another hour," you tell yourself). Sound familiar? What is wrong with starting a meeting fifteen minutes after the hour or forty-five minutes after the hour? There are sixty perfectly good minutes in an hour and we only use two points in time: 00 and 30. When someone wants to book a meeting with you at a time you're just ending another, try saying, "You know, I'm not available right at 1:00, but I can meet with you at 1:15." You'll end up being more focused and more creative, and you'll be a great role model for your teammates.

**Take Action:** The next time you book a meeting, make it fifteen or forty-five minutes after the hour to give you and all the other participants a chance to refocus, use the restroom, and be totally present in the meeting.

## Say "No" to Attending Every Meeting that You're Asked to Join

Having workloads that previously were spread among two or three people, many managers find themselves having more to do than can ever possibly be done. To try to fit everything in, managers frequently resort to overbooking their calendars. One business client of mine has teammates and customers throughout the country, making it necessary to have many telephone conference calls during the day. When she needs to attend two or more meetings that are being held at the same time, she utilizes some very creative tactics to be in two places at once. She first finds out the purpose of each meeting and exactly what is on both agendas. This way she can decide for herself the importance of attending the meetings. If one meeting is "informational only," she'll ask for the meeting notes or arrange to follow-up with one of the participants at a more convenient time. If she's required to provide information, she joins the call only when she's scheduled to talk. She makes herself available via pager or email should the participants have questions of her prior to or after she's on the call. If she's on another conference call, she can easily overlap and answer a question on email or excuse herself from the call to return the page. By utilizing this technique, she is able to attend more meetings and be a considerate team player, keeping herself available should she be needed.

When scheduled for more than one meeting at the same time, the following are some questions to ask to help you prioritize and decide which meeting to attend:

- What is the purpose of the meeting?
- What subjects are on the agenda?
- What will I give to the meeting? When/how much?
- What would happen if I didn't attend?
- Could a coworker represent me?
- What will I get from the meeting? When/how much?
- How else could I get the information (from where or whom)?

I recommend that for every meeting that you are asked to attend—whether or not you've got a schedule conflict—you ask yourself these questions. We just don't have the time anymore to attend every minute of every meeting. Of course, you must be sure to explain your absence to your teammates. Never assume that they don't need to know why you're not attending and *never, ever* leave them in the lurch. Always engage in proactive, open, and honest communication. A very effective technique is to contact the meeting facilitator or leader prior to the meeting. This gives you the opportunity to explain your schedule conflict, ask what information is needed from you for the meeting, how you can get the information you need after the meeting, and let them know how you can be contacted should they need to reach you during the meeting. Taking the time for this extra step will strengthen your relationships with your teammates and, at the same time, role model remarkable management skills!

*Take Action:* What schedule conflicts do you anticipate this coming week? Contact the key people to find out the answers to some of the questions above. You'll probably find that your presence isn't required for the entire meeting— allowing you to gain control of your schedule and get more of your work done!

## Say "No" to Becoming Tougher to Be a More "Effective" Manager

Do you know people who are nice when they are off work, yet tough as nails while on the job? Or better yet, do you know many managers who you dislike and then find out how friendly and funny they are off the job? You wonder why they can't bring some of that humanness into the workplace. Many managers feel that they need to distance themselves from their employees, be tough, and adhere rigidly to processes in order to be respected on the job. In reality, the most effective managers are the ones who develop relationships with their bosses, peers, and employees. Think about the managers who you most enjoyed working for— the ones you'll always remember (in a good way). Chances are they were not the tough managers, but the ones who showed that they cared, revealed their mistakes, made you laugh at times, and got along well with their bosses and coworkers.

The corporate culture is changing from autocratic to more democratic and the most successful managers are now the ones who build collaborative relationships with their employees. We see this cultural change in our society as well as in our workplace. Let's look at our children for a moment. When I was growing up, I did not sass or talk back to my parents. If they told me to do something, or not to do something, I pretty much obeyed them, no questions asked. They were the experts; they did the talking. Today, kids are quite different. They don't take "no" for an answer. You can't say, "because I told you so," and expect them to accept that as an answer. Kids today want to be included in decisions; they want—actually they demand—having their say into what's going on. They question authority. It's not that they're against authority per se, it's that they're unimpressed with authority.

We're seeing the same trends in the workplace. For years, management did all the talking; they were the experts. Employees did as they were told. No back-talking; no challenging; no discussing. Employees were happy to have a stable job—one that they would stay with for life. Today, employees want to have input and be valued for their ideas and contributions. They challenge and they ask questions. They want to work in *partnership* with you, not work in fear of you. With this new workplace culture, we now need to build *collaborative* relationships with our employees—a relationship that draws on both your employees' and your own ideas. The results are better solutions, engaged and motivated employees, and better, faster, cheaper end-results. The added bonus to you as a manager is that you won't work as hard because you've got creative, engaged employees who are eager to do the job.

Many of my business clients ask me, "How do I build a collaborative relationship with my employees?" A collaborative relationship is one in which both partners have a say, give and receive ideas and opinions, and make decisions. Here is a sample of some of the collaboration skills a manager can utilize:

- Active listening: listening without judgment, interruptions, or distractions
- Asking questions: drawing out ideas from employees instead of telling the employees what to do
- Identifying obstacles and challenges: mutually discovering what could get in employees' way to achieving successes
- Stretching employees without breaking them: encouraging them to maximize their strengths
- Celebrating minor and major accomplishments: acknowledging employees in ways that are meaningful to each one as an individual

I have found that by applying these new skills, managers get increased results from their employees, employees feel cared about and involved, and everyone becomes more passionate about their work.

**Take Action:** Top executives agree that listening is one of the key skills of an effective leader. How well do you listen? Ask a friend to talk to you for one minute about something that interests him or her. At the end of the minute, recite back what was said, using as many of your friend's exact words as possible. Then compare what you heard with what was actually said. Next, practice this with your employees—they'll be impressed with your increased attention!

## The Art of Saying "No"

I hope that this chapter has given you practical tips on how to say "No" and be a more productive manager. As with many managers before you, you may feel that the tactics that I have provided seem a bit out of reach or perhaps impossible to do. Yet many managers have had the courage to implement them and have lived to tell about their experiences! As a matter of fact, they cannot imagine working any other way anymore—they now have pieces of their lives back, feel more in control, and much more effective. I encourage you to work on these tactics a little at a time. You might start by scheduling your meetings at fifteen minutes past the hour instead of on the hour for a few weeks, and then add in practicing listening intently during one-on-one conversations with your employees. Next you can add scheduling breaks to regenerate in the middle of the day; and lastly, scheduling time each day to work on the business—time to create and plan. Little by little, you'll make these remarkable management skills a daily part of your work life. You'll be amazed at how much better you'll perform!

This is your life—it's happening now—make the choice to reclaim it today. As the quote at the beginning of the chapter declared, in order for things to change, you must change. In order for things to be different, you must be different.

## About
## Joyce Leonard

As a personal and business coach, Joyce Leonard draws upon her twenty-two years of experience in Fortune 500 companies, her Bachelor of Science degree in Organizational Behavior, and her personal life transformations. Having learned the challenges and realities of the fast-paced, results oriented business environment, she now teaches and coaches executives, directors, managers, project managers, team leaders, and supervisors in the areas of performance improvement, team building, improving communication and management skills, and attracting, engaging, and keeping the best employees—all geared to improving bottom line results. As a personal coach, she helps people achieve goals such as life-work balance, career changes, life transitions, improved communication and relationships, time and stress management, and weight loss. Joyce enjoys helping her clients focus better to produce results more quickly.

Joyce is a graduate of the University of San Francisco (B.S. in Organizational Behavior), a Certified TeleClass Leader, and a licensed trainer of the Personal Evolution program and Coaching Skills Clinic. She received her training from CoachU and Corporate Coach U. As a member of the International Coach Federation, CoachU, Coachville, and Corporate Coach University, she is knowledgeable, skilled, and linked to the most effective techniques and best practices available worldwide.

Joyce coaches individuals and teams who are ready to make changes in their work and personal lives. In a partnership setting, she challenges clients to discover the true successes they desire in their lives, anticipate obstacles and opportunities, and establish a concrete plan for change. Her unique qualities are her practical and realistic approaches to solving problems and reaching goals. Clients continually comment on her contagious enthusiasm and optimism. People have fun working with Joyce, in addition to learning more about themselves and how to reach their goals.

To find out how Joyce can help you at work and in your personal life, please contact her at 925-988-0920, send an email to Joyce@CoachJoyce.com, or visit her website at www.CoachJoyce.com. Joyce would love to hear of your successes; please contact her to let her know how you're doing! She'd be happy to coach you through a specific situation. Just mention this book and she'll give you a complementary 30-minute coaching session over the telephone.

# Excuses: the Opiate of the Unsuccessful
## Responsibility Revisited and Redefined

### By Schuyler Morgan

> "LIFE ULTIMATELY MEANS TAKING THE RESPONSIBILITY TO FIND
> THE RIGHT ANSWER TO ITS PROBLEMS AND TO FULFILL THE TASKS IT
> CONSTANTLY SETS FOR EACH INDIVIDUAL."
> ~ VICTOR FRANKL

What's going on? Business is at a crossroads. The CEO moral compass has been ignored. Toxic bosses still create unfriendly work environments. There is cynicism surrounding the mysterious and powerful boardrooms. Whistle-blowers have to play by "outsider" rules. Insurance costs now slam the executive suite. The barrage of bankruptcies and spate of corporate financial fraud has triggered the costliest business insurance rate hike in decades. Scandal and recession have cast a pall on the way executives go about leading their companies. Have we been caught "blind sided" at work?

Corporate, government, religious, and individual responsibility is in crisis. We have betrayed ourselves. We have learned to accept manipulation, threats, and greed from organizations' top talent. Accountability has been replaced with blame and excuses. We have become numb to the corporate abuse that drives character and integrity into the ground. False promises, pseudo relationships, lies, and deception have become the norm. We have sold ourselves short by believing the propaganda fed to us by the very people we "thought" we could trust.

Guess which company had the following to say in its 1999 annual report? "We...keep a keen eye on how prudent our employees are, and vigorously evaluate and control the risk involved in each of our activities." Here's more of a clue. When asked what it had been like working for that company, one member of the organization was reported to say earlier this year, "You keep up with Wall Street and make your numbers. By hook or by crook, you do it."

Would it surprise you to know that both of these quotes were about disgraced Texas energy company Enron? Given what we now know, which quote offers the more accurate picture of what actually went on there?

Not long ago, I attended a conference on business, competition, and where we are in the ongoing evolution of organizations. One of the speakers, a senior executive at a major multimedia company, caught my attention. He stood up in public in front of his peers and said, "Our way of doing business is broken."

Oddly enough, I found that admission enormously heartening. That executive said what most of us already know: that the old command-and-control structures, inspired by or inherited from the military, simply aren't effective anymore. It's based on winning at all costs with everyone acting on orders from the top down...no questions asked. Corporate cultures like that are definitely not fun or inspiring.

"THE NATURE OF HIERARCHICAL RELATIONSHIPS IS
FRAUGHT WITH DYSFUNCTION."
~ MATTHEW GILBERT

As we see the breakdown of trust in our corporate and political leaders, we see the very fabric of our capitalistic society fraying at the ends. Too often we see how brutally men and women suffer from the harsh cutbacks and relentless downsizing that rumble through corporate hierarchies. All these factors demonstrate just how wrong the conventional wisdom is for a competitive edge in today's turbulent age of paradox.

The need for change in the nature of work must not only be radical, it must also be prevalent in the way leaders lead organizations. We have come to recognize the human "etiquette" of the organization as a potent value driver, the lubricating oil of organizations for a radically different world of work. When we have to relate to, work with, and depend upon someone, nothing is more important than personal ethical virtues like honor, reliability, trustworthiness, emotional intelligence, and kindness. The time is upon us to revisit and redefine responsibility to build companies in which lives are lived honestly—a world of work where lives are integrated, not delegated.

Responsible managers are not relics from the past; rather, they are the wave of the future. When the pendulum of change in our society moves away from the entitlement mentality and back toward responsibility, they are the leaders who will shape our future. Since responsible managers will be the ones to produce consistent, high-quality results, they will emerge as the indispensable commodity in the corporate world. This chapter is written to help those who choose to become members of this elite group.

For over three decades, I have worked and coached in both old and new-economy businesses in the United States, Canada, Europe, and the United Kingdom. I have asked hundreds of business owners, managers, and executives, "Are some people more responsible than others?" The answer is a resounding "Yes." I have gone further and asked, "What tells you they are responsible?" I have heard a variety of answers. But as I look at the answers, some interesting patterns emerge. What is obvious is that:

- Responsibility is a choice. People either choose to be responsible, or they don't.
- Responsibility means making no excuses.
- Responsibility is relative. People are judged responsible according to the perspective of those who are doing the judging.

This chapter will focus on these three truths about responsibility in the workplace and how they impact the making of a Remarkable Manager.

## Responsibility is a Choice

*"Life is a grindstone. But whether it grinds us down or polishes us up depends on us."*
*~ L. Thomas Holdcroft*

You can hire for responsibility. You can nurture and coach responsibility. You can develop skills, understanding, and attitudes that make it more likely that responsible people will act responsibly. But as much as we want responsible workers, we can't *make* workers responsible, because responsibility is a choice.

No matter what the circumstances, you still have the power to choose what you think and what you do. This basic truth is one of the most empowering discoveries a person can make. The power of this understanding is brilliantly revealed in the writings of Victor Frankl, a psychiatrist, who while imprisoned at the Nazi death camp Auschwitz, somehow found the strength to survive under horrifying experiences.

Frankl watched many in the camp retreat into the past and into despair. Frankl found his strength in his hopes and dreams for the future. He took the camp's difficulties as a test of his inner strength and found within himself what he would later call "the last of the human freedoms"—the basic freedom that even his Nazi tormentors could not take from him. He had the freedom to choose how to react to all they did to him. And he realized it was his responsibility to make the most of his life. And he committed himself to not giving in to his captors, to win in the end—to survive.

Human beings have the freedom to choose how they will respond to everything that affects them. We have the freedom to choose what we will think, say, and do. We can decide. In fact, this insight—if it becomes a driving force in our life, a habit—may be one of the strongest predictors of our success—and of those we lead.

## Responsibility: The Core of "Emotional Intelligence"

*"EVERY MAN IS LIKE THE COMPANY HE IS WONT TO KEEP."*

~ EURIPIDES

Awareness is the key ingredient in responsibility. To act responsibly, a person must first be aware of her situation and feelings and then exercise her power to control the response.

For years psychologists and educators have looked to intelligence quotient (IQ) as the great determiner of success. But the exceptions to the rule have always puzzled us. Why didn't the class valedictorian end up being one of the most successful? Why do some very mediocre performers on the Scholastic Aptitude Test do so well in college or become such great successes later in their careers?

Some of the answers can be found in the statistics used to validate the power of intelligence and our inability to measure other things. The recent work on emotional intelligence (EQ) is believed by some to hold promise of producing better predictions. John Mower, the Yale psychologist who coined the term *emotional intelligence,* and Daniel Goleman, who popularized it, describe a variety of qualities that they believe have more power in predicting success in life than does IQ. Goleman states, "When it comes to predicting people's success, braininess as measured by IQ and standardized achievement tests may actually matter less than the qualities of the mind, once thought of as 'character' before the word began to sound quaint." This character could also be called a sense of responsibility. In fact, responsibility may well be at the core of emotional intelligence.

## The Critical Role of Optimism

*"I KNOW WORRYING MUST BE EFFECTIVE BECAUSE ALMOST NOTHING I WORRIED ABOUT EVER HAPPENED."*

*~ WILL ROGERS*

Another strong predictor of success that is strongly associated with responsibility is optimism. Martin Seligman, a University of Pennsylvania psychologist, has found that optimism, as measured through an instrument he devised, is a fairly accurate predictor of how well a person will succeed in school, sports, and certain kinds of work. He has successfully predicted the accomplishments of salespeople with his tests of optimism. Seligman found that when they fail, optimists most often attribute the failure to something they can control, not to some innate weakness that they are helpless to overcome. The optimism comes from the person's sense of power over her environment, her confidence in her ability to make changes, even in her own life.

When optimists succeed, they explain it in terms of permanent causes: traits, abilities, and personality. Pessimists explain success as based on chance or temporary conditions, feelings, moods or efforts. Optimists therefore believe good things are likely to happen again. The optimists' confidence is self-reinforcing since it keeps them trying, thinking, and problem solving longer than others. A lack of confidence is also self-reinforcing. For example, the salesman who is pessimistic about his sales call and therefore doesn't make the call, has no chance to succeed.

People are more likely to act responsibly when they are self-aware, understand that they do have the power to control their emotional and behavioral responses to the world around them, and believe that they can change the factors that are limiting their success. It may be that like EQ, optimism is driven by responsibility, or that people with high EQ and optimism are more likely to be responsible.

## Responsibility Means No Excuses

*"Do or not do. There is no try."*

~ Yoda

Excuses are the opiate of the unsuccessful. Just as realizing that they have the freedom to choose empowers people, the willingness to make excuses makes them victims. There appears to be a worldwide search for excuses today. People blame the way they are on childhood experiences, a bad teacher, the system, genetics, or a lack of information. The problem with making excuses is that it can become a habit, and once you have the habit it becomes easier to find an excuse than to try hard to change your condition. You become more of a victim than a center of power and influence. You become disempowered.

The habit of making excuses produces people who believe in their helplessness and victimization. If they take responsibility, it is limited to factors they can easily control, such as common sense, completing forms, or asking for clarification for goal setting.

Excuses, pessimism, and helplessness go hand in hand. The excuses are the symptom and the pessimism and helplessness the underlying habit and feeling. Whatever the relationship, the elements are generally found together and are the enemies of personal responsibility, success, and remarkable management.

Choosing to blame someone or something for your problems brings some relief—from accountability, from facing the challenge of the problem yourself, and from acknowledging your contribution to the problem. In other words, by not taking responsibility you disconnect yourself from the world you live in. This act dehumanizes and disempowers you, producing short-term relief and long-term problems. There is difficulty in taking responsibility. Which helps explain why responsibility is less prevalent than most of us would like. When you connect and commit to the world by taking responsibility, you are faced with tough choices and the discomfort that goes with them. The rewards, however, come over the long run in terms of confidence, respect, and a general feeling of empowerment.

## Responsibility as Defined on Two Dimensions

> "HOLD YOURSELF RESPONSIBLE FOR A HIGHER STANDARD THAN
> ANYBODY EXPECTS OF YOU. NEVER EXCUSE YOURSELF."
> ~ HENRY WARD BEECHER

Practically speaking, responsibility can be defined on two dimensions represented by two small words: *to* and *for.* For example, as we mature, we learn that we have responsibility *to* our family, our friends, our community, our society, and ourselves. We also learn that we are responsible *for* our actions, our words, the use of our talents, those who need our help, and each of the things we own.

Most people think they are responsible. For instance, less responsible people may take responsibility for activities such as showing up, doing their best, or completing the task. People who are pointed out as being more responsible, however, take responsibility for results. They take responsibility for the outcomes of their actions even when the results are less than desirable. And when they know what the goal is, they work hard to achieve it even in the face of great difficulties.

The following story helps to bring home this powerful distinction. Imagine being a world-renowned public speaker who has found that an important factor in his success is getting himself and his handout materials to the client on time. In fact, this is so important, his company hires one person whose primary responsibility is for getting him and the materials to every event on time and in good condition. Nearly a decade ago, he was on his way to a speaking engagement outside the United States. He describes the following conversation with his previous personal assistant for these events:

"My plane stopped in Chicago and I called the office to check on a few things. As I walked to the phone, I had a horrible déjà vu experience. Eight years before, I had been going to this same conference to be the keynote speaker. I had stopped in Chicago then, too. I had called the office to talk to Linda, the woman in charge of the handout materials. I asked if my materials had arrived in Toronto. 'Don't worry,' was the response, 'I sent them out six days ago.' 'Have they gotten there yet?' I asked. 'I sent them Federal Express. They guaranteed to be there in two days,' was the not so reassuring reply."

Surely Linda felt responsible. She felt responsible for getting the right information (address, date, contact person, number, and type of materials). She probably felt responsible for choosing the right shipping container, packing the box to protect the materials, and getting it to Federal Express early enough to allow some cushion for a timely delivery. But, as the conversation shows, she had not followed through to ensure results. The story continues:

"Recently, with the memory of that former phone call running through my mind, I approached the new phone call with some trepidation. When I reached my assistant, Amy, I asked, 'Are my materials there yet?' 'Yes, Alicia got them three days ago,' she said, 'but when I called she told me there would be 400 extra people at the speech. Don't worry, though, she's gotten the extras too. In fact, she seemed a bit unsure about the number so I asked her if the number was fixed. She said not exactly because people can register at the door. Given this, I was afraid that 400 wouldn't be enough, so I sent 600 just to be safe. By the way, she asked me if you wanted the materials handed out ahead of time. I told her usually you do. But since this is a new speech, I wasn't sure. So we agreed that she will hand them out ahead of time, unless you tell her not to do that. I have her phone number where she can be reached tonight, if you want her to do something different.' "

Here's a simple question: Which of these two women, Amy or Linda, would you like to have working for you? The answer is obvious. You would like Amy, because she takes responsibility for results. She knows that results are critical and she won't rest until she delivers them.

### Results vs. Activities

*"IF YOU DON'T TAKE CHARGE OF SHAPING YOUR OWN DESTINY,*
*OTHERS WILL APPLY THEIR AGENDA TO YOU."*
*~ ERIC ALLENBAUGH*

Leaders generally agree that they want people to take responsibility for results. And they generally agree that their greatest frustrations come from people who focus their responsibility on activities. The problem is that too many managers manage as though they want people to be responsible for activities rather than results.

If you really wanted to focus on results you want from a position, remember that responsible people need to know what results you're after, then all you have to do is get out of their way. So what is important is to focus your hiring activities on finding out about the character of the people you are considering. Try to assess their understanding of the importance of results, maybe their EQ or level of optimism or ability to handle discomfort in the pursuit of goals. Determine who are the result producers. Do not focus primarily on the activities they have been involved with in the past. And focus the training on the results you want, how to evaluate whether they've been achieved, and then and only then, on activities that "usually" lead to those results. Unfortunately, all too few of these statements are descriptive of common management practices.

To truly create a responsible organization, the way you hire and focus management on developing the skills, attitudes, and abilities forms the foundation of responsibility. Hire and develop people who are prepared to change their activities when they realize that the desired results aren't happening. Truly responsible people aren't very happy if they are only given responsibility for activities. It takes them out of the game and does not allow them to be creative, exercise judgment, make decisions, or feel that they've really made a contribution.

## Responsibility and Maturity

*"A MATURE PERSON IS ONE WHO KNOWS THAT*
*'NO' IS A COMPLETE SENTENCE."*
*~ANONYMOUS*

Over time the challenge becomes balancing all the constituencies of our responsibility. Often our responsibilities to others compete with one another and with our responsibility to ourselves. For example, we stay late at work to complete an important project even though we'd like to be working out or at home with the family.

The same could be said for the super manager. Remember, as you take on new responsibilities, you should try to shed old ones. This doesn't mean that you should walk away from them. Rather, you should plan to develop others who will have the capability to and are prepared to take on your old responsibilities as you take on new ones. The truly responsible manager has the maturity to say "no" to the request, if they can't delegate, in order to be truly responsible for quality results.

The president of a West Coast family lumber company was describing his hectic life and some challenges in the accounting reports. He was asked, "What does the chief financial officer say about that?" He replied, "I am the CFO." "What about the chief information officer?" was the next question. "I'm also the CIO," was his answer. This very responsible, dedicated, second-generation president of a $30-million company still held every job he had ever had in the company since he joined it. After coaching, he learned how to develop other people's talents and give away jobs.

How many people do you know who have trouble saying "no" or have trouble developing others and nurturing and delegating responsibility? These skills along with setting personal goals and priorities are critical for people with a well-developed sense of responsibility.

This relationship between responsibility and our ability to assess (to be self-aware, observe, and interpret what we see, hear, and feel), to make decisions relative to what we are sensing and what actions we should take, and to solve problems is critical. At some point, the tasks we are given or are expected to perform involve uncertainty and judgment. They cannot be completed successfully just by following rules, protocols, and procedures.

Achieving results, whatever the obstacles, requires persistence, perspective, and judgment. Leaders win when they delegate to people who will take responsibility for the results. The willingness to take on and the ability to complete undefined tasks when the desired results are clearly stated are defining characteristics of the people we regularly call responsible.

## Responsibility is Relative

"PEOPLE ONLY SEE WHAT THEY ARE PREPARED TO SEE."
~ RALPH WALDO EMERSON

A common assumption is that more responsible people take on more responsibility to others. However, in reality, being responsible to more constituencies does not necessarily mean that we are being more responsible. Sometimes giving up some of our responsibility to one or more of our constituencies is the most responsible thing to do.

The highly successful business executive who spends long hours at work, is forever on the road, and regularly misses family events may be considered less responsible by his or her spouse and children, while the chairmen of the board may see the same person as very responsible.

People judge the responsibility of others by whom (or what) they are responsible to and what they take responsibility for. If you appear to be responsible to those I believe you should be responsible to, and if you take responsibility for what I believe you should take responsibility for, I will judge you as being responsible.

Notice that my judgment regarding your responsibility can be affected by a number of things. These include:

- The congruence between my beliefs regarding responsibility (to and for) and my interpretation of your behavior.
- The congruence between your feelings of responsibility (to and for), the decisions you make, and your behavior.
- The congruence of my beliefs regarding responsibility (to and for) and yours.

A good place to start developing responsibility in an organization is to get people on the same wavelength regarding whom or what to be responsible to and what to be responsible for (the organization, the customer, and to other employees).

## Building a River of Responsibility

*"WE GENERALLY BEHAVE AS IF OUR'S IS THE ONLY REALITY THAT COUNTS AND THEN WONDER WHY WE'RE HAVING SO MUCH TROUBLE GETTING ALONG WITH OTHERS."*

*~ANONYMOUS*

Think of the power of a river. That power comes from the volume of water, the pull of gravity, and the focus provided by the riverbanks. The volume of water comes from many small sources, all-running in the same direction. The pull of gravity provides drive and force as the water moves toward its goal, the ocean. The banks provide boundaries that concentrate the flow and give it more force and power.

Unfortunately, many organizations are more like puddles or lakes than powerful rivers. They may be tranquil and peaceful, but they aren't going anywhere. They do not collect and concentrate the efforts of the entire organization, or have the pull of a clear sense of purpose, or the boundaries needed to focus their efforts to allow them to go over and around, under or through, the obstacles they encounter.

To build a powerful river of responsibility to customers in your organization you must follow these steps:

- Get everyone committed to producing the results customers want.
- Provide focus by:
  - ~ Carefully selecting the customers and needs you will serve.
  - ~ Creating strategies that focus on providing value to select customers.
  - ~ Aligning structures, systems, processes, and culture with the strategy.
  - ~ Getting everyone involved in improving value to the customer and managing each customer interaction.

When we consider developing responsibility to the organization, we should focus on four major areas:

- Creating an organization to which people choose to be responsible.
- Developing an understanding of the results organizations must achieve to be successful and what each individual can do to affect those results.
- Creating reward and recognition systems that are consistent with organizational goals and strategies.
- Developing an organization of results-oriented problem solvers.

Developing responsibility to the organization starts with a simple question: What characteristics of an organization would cause you to choose to be responsible or committed to it? After asking this question of hundreds of people in different companies and in different positions, their answers have been surprisingly similar.

People would choose to be responsible to an organization that:

- Has a clear, meaningful sense of direction.
- Has (and lives by) values they can respect.
- Respects them and their contributions.
- Has a compatible culture.
- Is a source of pride.
- Enables them to do challenging and meaningful work.

## Having and Living By Values People Respect

*"Do not say things. What you are stands over you the while, and thunders so that I cannot hear what you say to the contrary."*
*~ Ralph Waldo Emerson*

Core values may drive a company's strategy and decisions and may be major determiners of its success. But they are not the only values companies are judged by. There are a number of other values, real or imagined, long-term or short-term, that affect whether people will choose to be responsible to a given organization.

Most people believe that a person's or a company's behavior is in some way reflective of their values. Human beings have a strong tendency to read intent into behavior.

As unproductive as it is to make assumptions about values or intentions, people do it anyway. Employees regularly infer the values of an organization from its behavior, and the values they infer would shock most of those businesses' leaders.

For example, one excitable entrepreneur has a hard time containing herself in a discussion. When she gets excited about an idea, she blurts it out, often while someone else is talking. Members of her executive team have lots of praise for her intellect, insight, and charisma. However, they also say, "She doesn't really value what we have to say," because of her "butting in." Of course, her behavior is a problem, but their diagnosis of the cause is incorrect.

The entrepreneur, with coaching, identified some group process skills and learned some rules (for example, don't talk out of turn). Now she doesn't butt in, and because she acts as if she cares for and respects the input of her colleagues, they think she does.

All too often, companies espouse values but give little behavioral evidence that they exist. This really doesn't fool anyone. Workers are much more apt to believe what you do than what you say if the two are inconsistent. When you live the values in the culture, you will have no problem finding people who will choose to be responsible to your organization.

People want to work in environments where they and their contributions are respected. When there is no respect, each day is demeaning. There is little sense of self-worth and contribution. Confident, optimistic, capable people will not stay in an environment that offers little respect. Unfortunately, much of our workaday world does not let us see the real potential of our colleagues. Allowing people to participate in or even to play a key role in important things is the sincerest sign of respect.

When people work for an organization they are ready to commit themselves to, know what results they must produce, have the requisite information, and have a proper reward and recognition system, the only challenge left is providing people with the basic skills and knowledge that will enable them to create the results: problem solving and decision-making.

With this in mind, the focus of coaching for responsibility is on the critical roles of judgment and problem solving in producing results, and on providing in-depth instruction in the artful science of solving problems with individuals, teams, and communication in organizations.

## Corporate Personality

*"THINKING ABOUT CORPORATE CULTURE MIGHT SOUND SOMEWHAT 'TOUCHY FEELY,' BUT I WOULD ARGUE THAT FEW CHARACTERISTICS ARE MORE IMPORTANT TO A COMPANY'S SUCCESS."*
~ THE MOTLEY FOOL, A FINANCIAL WEBSITE

Fortunately there are companies that receive consistently high marks for employee satisfaction, have low rates of turnover, and earn impressive financial returns. They have integrated corporate values and personal values into a way of doing business that honors the need for both. The recipe for success is slightly different for each, but they all share characteristics that make them stand out in a crowd. This is where the nitty-gritty of workplace culture comes in.

In short, workplace culture is defined by a company's mission, goals, and values and by how those things influence the working environment itself and the behaviors of those who work there. It's basically what differentiates working for one company from working for another. From the pressed-suit rigidity of Wall Street to the "anything goes" philosophy of dot.coms (at least in the early days), each company has its own spoken and unspoken rules of conduct, further influenced by societal standards and gender conditioning of what is and isn't okay.

But even companies in the same business can have very diverse dispositions. To get a better sense of your workplace culture, think of it as having a personality. Is it loose or rigid, fun or serious, caring or cold? Could it be characterized as a racecar driver, or mother hen, a stuffy patriarch, an absent-minded professor? Is it more like Gordon Gecko, the character in the movie *Wall Street,* ready to eat someone's lunch at a moment's notice, or like good-guy banker Jimmy Stewart in *It's a Wonderful Life?* Your company's personality plays a significant role in today's competitive market for attracting and retaining responsible talent.

## Some Final Thoughts

*"We're talking about our jobs becoming a place where we continue to grow as human beings and, in turn, to grow the organization along with us."*
~Matthew Gilbert

How we communicate at our jobs (verbally and non-verbally) is influenced by what is and isn't valued in our company's particular culture. People communicate all the time, at many levels, in many situations, and for many purposes. Sometimes this communication consists of a hello when we walk through the office door in the morning; other times it goes to the heart of a company's mission, how it envisions its role in the lives of its employees and in the community it serves. The emphasis in this chapter has been on the deceptive complexity that underlies what we say, how we say it, and why we say it.

Much has been written about the sorry state of our workplaces, and it's true that years of abuse and neglect have led to fearful, cynical environments where communication is used more often as a weapon than a tool. It's clear that for companies to meet the challenges of the twenty-first century, they will have to cultivate an atmosphere of trust and learning where people treat one another with compassion, caring, and respect. We are facing some difficult choices about how to create a future that works—personally, economically, culturally, and collectively. What values will guide us?

The discussion in this chapter may even nudge corporate decision-makers to rethink their approach to employee and customer relations, and it may help bring a little more peace to your working life. What I really hope to have accomplished is to show what the workplace could feel like if a true spirit of community was present, created by a committed group of people who value each other as they work toward achieving a common vision. As the walls between us come down and our true humanity emerges, as we start "walking our talk," that potential will surely become a reality.

## About
## Schuyler Morgan

Schuyler Morgan, Professional Certified Coach (PCC), is the Founder and President of Catalytic Business Coaching, a combined network of coaches and consultants who offer an array of services to industries worldwide, spanning all aspects of Enterprise Risk for Business Continuity and Crisis Management. Schuyler's reputation precedes her, because of her remarkable skill with leading high impact teams, using the coach approach for peak performance. Since 9/11, she has developed a high impact Executive and Team Crisis Leadership model to fill the missing link in contemporary organizational development for today's complex eWorld, and for leading under fire.

Ms. Morgan delivers her revolutionary eCulture Leadership coaching to individuals, entrepreneurs, teams, and organizations' top talent. She coaches them to radically shift their thinking and break out of their comfort zones, an absolute requirement for a competitive edge in this turbulent age of paradox. Her alertness to cutting edge issues and trends keeps her coaching sharp and focused.

She recently Co-founded Finishing Up – A Contemporary Finishing School with Personal Coaching for Professionals. For anyone who wants to realize their potential and avoid the pitfalls of our eCulture Age of Paradox, this trailblazing venture reminds us that character issues get people hired as well as fired. The absence of strong character may cause damage to teams, to quality, to reputations and the enterprise at large. The advantages of contemporary individual leadership, manners, and etiquette are that they serve as a guide to confidence, enjoyment, civility, and dignity for profiting in the age we live.

Schuyler, a sought-after professional speaker, is often seen as a formidable wit and an irresistible combination of iconoclasm and convention. She doesn't give you rules; she gives you perspective. For those who have stumbled through life wondering if there are any easy answers, the happy news is, Schuyler helps you find them.

She has authored the booklet *The Art of Recognition*, is a contributing author of the books *A Guide to Getting It: Self-Esteem* and *A Guide to Getting It: Achieving Abundance* and is busy working on her book *Too Busy to Love, Too Tired to Care: Juggling Work and Life in Uncertain and Unreasonable Times*. She also has numerous articles appearing in publications in the U.S. and Canada. She is an alumna of Leadership America, and is past Editor-in-Chief of the International Coach Federation's Organizational Coach eJournal.

Ms. Morgan is in a unique position to coach individuals and organizations toward their potential by combining her knowledge of human dynamics and high performance organizational cultures. She seems particularly able to understand people and the human factor in situations, especially in today's demanding fast-paced environments. Schuyler has the energy, confidence, and spirit to initiate in all environments, and to influence outcomes, a necessary sign of authentic leadership abilities. These abilities are well developed in her coaching approach. She blends the strength of maturity with the enthusiasm, vigor, and spontaneity of youth.

Ms. Morgan resides in Oakland, California. To contact her, phone: 510-653-6868 or email her at Schuyler@eCultureCoach.com. Please visit: www.CatalyticBizCoaching.com , www.eCultureCoach.com and www.FinishingUp.com.

# A Leadership Culture: The Heart of High Performance Organizations

## By Shariann Tom, John Vercelli & Mai Vu

The opportunity for significant improvement is readily available to every company with the courage to delve into the most mysterious aspect of business, the human being. Every person has the capacity for outstanding and, sometimes, astounding performance. This chapter proposes how to get that performance daily from every level in the company.

A simple, yet profound idea is at the heart of organizations that realize that potential: **Everyone is a leader, all of the time**. A company where every individual is a leader for their segment of the business, regardless of job title or position, is practicing a leadership culture and will build customer loyalty, and, therefore, market share.

Respected authors such as Warren Bennis, Jim Collins, and John Kotter have studied the characteristics of leadership and culture that lead to high performance and sustained results. The high rate of change and the complexity of the global economy require a new way for everyone in the organization to act. Warren Bennis captures both the direction and passion behind this:

"Our observations have taught us that no single leader can save the day. Truly successful leadership today requires teams, collaboration, diversity, innovation, and cooperation. Leadership has begun to take on a new dimension. The leadership we are seeking is one that is empowering, supportive, visionary, problem-solving, creative, and shared."[1]

Mr. Bennis continues and offers a solution,

"The failures of our corporations demand leadership qualities from every staff member, every secretary, every salesperson, every accounts payable clerk, and every CEO, so as to catalyze enthusiasm, encourage risk taking, and create breakthroughs in innovation. The future will work only when each of us *makes it work*."[2]

Mr. Bennis is calling each of us to step into leadership regardless of our position. This is particularly poignant in light of the recent collapse of Enron and Arthur Andersen. In Jim Collins' book, *Good to Great*, he defines "level 5 leaders" as those who, among other things, respond to challenges by asking, "Who are the right people to address this?" rather than with a directive. These leaders realize that people—at every level—truly make the difference between adequate performance and sustained outstanding performance.

This is a shift from the recent days of Total Quality Management and Re-engineering, where the focus was on business processes. The focus is again on the human side of the equation. This return to the human factor does not throw out the gains of those initiatives, but rather finds new sources of improvement. We believe that there are significant untapped resources waiting to be unleashed in each and every person in organizations, and that building a leadership culture will realize that potential.

## Living In a Leadership Culture

There are several unique aspects to the working relationships in a company practicing a leadership culture. These aspects routinely occur throughout every day, whether in a staff meeting, project meeting, performance review, or a sales conversation.

**Giving and receiving full attention.** Successful collaboration starts with listening. To listen requires setting aside one's agenda and placing full attention on the other. In a meeting, genuine curiosity about one person's position leads to questions and inquiry. This generates the most information enabling the group to generate the best decision, plan, or solution.

**Task and process are balanced.** Task accomplishment and attention to the process are given appropriate amounts of time. Both are needed for success. Overemphasis of task focus leads to ineffective implementation, usually because there is inadequate commitment from all parties. Every decision includes an emotional component that needs to be addressed. As a former engineer, I can attest to this even within the most technical issues.

**Learning is always part of the agenda.** Every challenge, issue, and problem is seen as an opportunity to learn. This is another aspect of balancing task and process. The learning serves both the individual and the company. The individual gains more than just new skills, they move past limiting beliefs, test assumptions, and make distinct choices rather than react to circumstances. For the company, the collective knowledge and capability expands, thus ensuring the company's competitive strength.

**Celebrate success and failure.** When learning is valued, people are willing to go beyond their comfort zone. This lifts a major block to innovation. Success and failure are celebrated equally because they represent two aspects of learning. A willingness to ask for help is an offshoot of this characteristic. Asking for help can be interpreted as failing, so people do not ask. Outside of a leadership culture, asking is considered a sign of vulnerability and lack of intelligence. In a leadership culture, people happily ask, and as a result, contribute with lower stress and increased morale.

**Focus on goal/desired outcomes.** Assigning blame, complaining, falling victim to circumstances are common themes in typical meetings. These will still occasionally occur in a leadership culture. However, those issues are not allowed to take over. Someone will call attention to this unproductive habit (process focus) and redirect the conversation to the desired outcome. In essence, creating a vision that everyone can focus on leads to a plan to create the best possible result, rather than getting stuck in the current situation.

**Independence and Interdependence are balanced.** We are each unique and all are part of a whole. Emphasizing one over the other is less productive. Individual mission, vision, and values have a place. They are the source of motivation and personal satisfaction that pay back at a deeper level than salary, stock, or bonuses can ever achieve. The greatest fulfillment comes with serving a larger purpose that is an extension of what is important to each person. Recruitment and retention are easy when the individual and company's mission, vision, and values are in alignment.

While any one of these may sound relatively inconsequential, together they create a culture of innovation, accountability, commitment, loyalty, and results. Leadership culture is not a destination, but a practice. At Innerworks Solutions, we fall out of a leadership culture essentially every moment and pull ourselves back every moment. We are better examples of the tenacious commitment to living a leadership culture than we are an example of the ideal. Although living a leadership culture is simple and the rewards are great, it is not easy.

## The Business Case for a Leadership Culture

Nearly every company expresses the belief that "Employees are our most important resource," or some similar sentiment. While this is intuitive, what is the connection to profit?

Innerworks Solutions trains managers to work with employees as leaders. The workshop begins with a simple exercise that exposes a strong belief in the centrality of the human in a business's success. First, we ask managers, "What does your company do to manage performance and develop employees?" The responses include: company mission; annual and quarterly company goals that are translated to department goals and objectives (MBO, Hoshin planning); salary and benefits, bonuses, stock, recognition programs, annual performance reviews, and training programs. These responses are recorded on a flip chart surrounding an oval that represents an individual employee. Personal mission and vision, values, emotions, attitudes, and beliefs reside inside the "egg." Figure 1 captures the common responses.

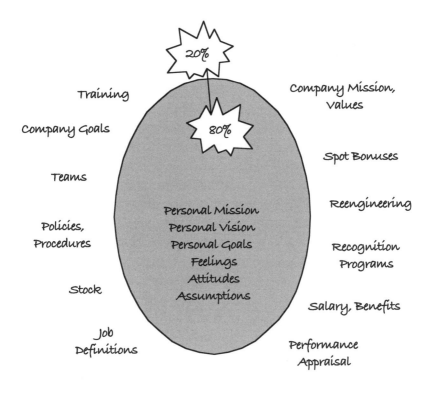

FIGURE 1. MANAGING AND DEVELOPING EMPLOYEES

Then we ask, "On a 100% scale, what is the relative influence on performance of the items outside the egg and those inside the egg?" The most common answer is 80% inside, though some put it as high as 90% or as low as 50%. Intuitively, managers know that what goes on inside each of their employees has significant impact on their performance, and consequently, business performance. Unfortunately, many managers are unsure or uncomfortable working with an employee at this level. Helping managers engage with their employees on the internal elements is a key to building a leadership culture and is addressed more fully later in the chapter.

## Another Human Link: Customer Satisfaction and Loyalty

Assuming there is a sound business model, sustained and increasing profit arises from market share. The company with the larger market share has the opportunity for higher gross margins than competitors. Being the technology leader is an increasingly difficult strategy for gaining market share because today's innovation quickly becomes tomorrow's commodity. Total quality management, six-sigma, and just-in-time production have been commonly practiced for the past ten to fifteen years to keep costs low. Innovation and low prices certainly contribute to market share, but achieving a competitive advantage increasingly depends on giving the customer a great experience. Eventually, some human being at the customer's company interacts with a human being at your company. Every one of these events is an opportunity to build customer loyalty.

Customer loyalty includes three elements:
1.  Customers report high satisfaction.
2.  Customers will repurchase.
3.  Customers recommend your company to others.

So, customer loyalty is essential for increasing market share. Without it, the company has to replace customers to even maintain market share, which costs more than keeping existing customers. The critical link lies between the employee and customer loyalty. Figure 2 links profit to individual performance.

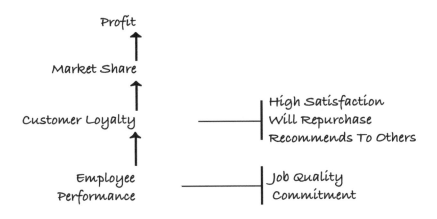

FIGURE 2. THE VALUE CHAIN

Let's assume that your employees know what you expect of them, have the tools needed for that job, and that their skills, knowledge, and talent match the job requirements.[3] As a manager, you have done everything to ensure performance adequate to meet customer expectations, the base for customer loyalty. Unfortunately, customers can get that level of performance from your competitors. We believe that getting customers to repurchase and to recommend your company requires a high level of performance that can only come from committed employees. Committed employees do the job as if they owned the company and give customers an experience that builds loyalty. Compliant employees—those who adequately perform the job with no emotional investment—leave the customer with a bland (at best) experience.

W. Edwards Deming, the father of the quality movement, claimed that the system determined at least 80% of job performance. The other 20%, determined by the individual, is the critical difference for building a company's long-term success. Deming also said that managers are responsible for the system. Now, engendering commitment is added to the list. Managers cannot force commitment or devise an incentive plan for it. They must be willing to work with the elements inside the egg to help each individual find it. Once they do, a leadership culture will take root.

## Foundations of a Leadership Culture

This section covers the definitions, assumptions, and principles that are the foundation of a leadership culture.

### Definitions

**Leader:** Kevin Cashman, executive coach and author, defines leadership as "authentic self-expression that creates value."[4] A leader also takes responsibility for his or her impact. This applies to everyone in an organization, regardless of job title. They are clear about their personal mission, vision, and values and how they align to those of the organization.

**Culture:** The combination of behavioral norms, shared values, and unique language for a group.[5]

Cultures contain a set of assumptions that influence how people interpret information.

### Assumptions

- **Each person is creative, resourceful, and whole.**[6] Innerworks Solutions recommends this as the starting point in any interaction, whether with an employee, colleague, boss, or customer. To assure this assumption is true, we need only support each other in discovering the answers we have within. As a result, the employee wants to be challenged to go beyond what they think they might believe they are capable. They don't need the leader to solve problems or take care of them. While it may be easy to imagine treating a respected colleague this way, imagine approaching everyone this way.

- **Everyone wants to contribute to a purpose larger than him or her.** We are fortunate to be living in a society where the first two levels of Maslow's hierarchy of needs are met for a large percentage of the population. The need for social acceptance and esteem can often be met by working in a well managed company. So, the level of self-actualization can be tapped as the primary source of high performance.

- **Everyone wants to do a good job.** Social acceptance and esteem can be achieved through one's job performance. According to Maslow, these needs are inherent in each of us.

- **Commitment comes from within.** Choice leads to commitment. You *cannot* coerce, cajole, motivate, logically argue, or threaten a person into commitment. You *can* get a person to reflect and choose, which leads to commitment.

- **Significant alignment exists between the company's and the individual's mission, vision, and values, though it may be unconscious.** Everyone in a company desires success for themselves and for the company. We often discover that so-called difficult employees are just frustrated by the systemic blocks to doing a good job. In our coaching work, we help individuals clarify their personal mission and values and generally discover that they align nicely with the company mission and values. The individual employee's attitude shifts toward more enthusiasm for their work once they realize that doing a good job for the company is inherently rewarding for them. For those employees with little alignment between their mission and the company's, it is best for all parties that they leave.

- **Learning faster than your competitors is the only** *sustainable competitive advantage.* This brings us back to the business case. When humans are the critical success factor, then how quickly individuals and the company learn determines success.[7] Leaders are learners. They follow their passion, try new things, fail, then try something new. However, a leader as the lone cowboy is past. Leaders operate as a member of a team or community, dedicated to their growth. They challenge each other to continue learning.

Principles

- **Everyone is a leader, all of the time.** This is true literally of every person in every position in the company. This extends beyond the workday to the roles each of us plays in the community.
- **Take 100% responsibility.**[8] Peter Koestenbaum explains the importance of this concept in a Fast Company magazine interview, "Taking personal responsibility for getting others to implement strategy is the leader's key polarity. It's the existential paradox of holding yourself 100% responsible for the fate of your organization, on the one hand, and assuming absolutely no responsibility for the choices made by other people, on the other hand. That applies to your children too. You are 100% responsible for how your children turn out. And you accomplish that by teaching them that they are 100% responsible for how they turn out." At less than 100% responsibility, we believe we are the victim of the prevailing circumstances and blame others for our situation. Over 100%, we become martyrs. Finding others lacking, we believe we must get the job done. We alienate the very people we need for success, and ultimately fail.

- **Together we have the best answer.** In a complex, fast moving world we need to tap the knowledge and experience of every employee. Jim Collins' level 5 leaders put this into practice by asking who are the best people to address a given challenge. Deming extolled the need to have those closest to the work involved in making improvements because they know the most about it. The manager living this principle starts with inquiring about what the employee thinks or has tried before making a recommendation.

- **Listening provides value.** This principle is offered in balance to problem solving. I was recognized as an engineer and promoted into management because I solved problems. If adequate performance and average customer satisfaction is sufficient, problem solving managers are all that is needed. If you want customer loyalty, spend 80% of your time listening. I was promoted from supervisor to director in four years because I believed in my employees and was genuinely curious about them and their ideas. So, I listened, asked many questions, and acted to make my employees successful.

- **Consciously designed relationships are the most productive.** Like listening, effective work relationships are a two-way process. To borrow the ecological concept of interdependence, each of our success is tied to the success of others. In other words, if I make you successful, I will contribute to my success and vice-versa. While I didn't consciously realize it, I practiced this principle. Making my employees successful led to my promotion. In most organizations, there is a formal process that addresses the manager-employee relationship. In practice, this can be as simple as asking what an employee needs from his or her manager. Of course, the manager explains what is needed of the employee, as well. However,

Innerworks Solutions recommends conducting similar conversations in virtually all partnerships.

- **Create value in every interaction.** There is no time-out. Another way this has been expressed: "In life there is no dress rehearsal." Specifically, this assumes every person interacts with each other as leaders. They hold each other with high expectations, hold each other accountable, tell each other hard truths, hold all of the above assumptions as true, and act on the principles of a leadership culture. These types of interactions occur all day, every day, in chance encounters in the hall, in formal meetings, and over lunch.

## Remarkable Management Skills

In day-to-day practice, a leadership culture is expressed in co-active coaching skills.[9] Innerworks Solutions has adapted the skills and training developed for professional coaches to a corporate setting. As culture comprises a set of behavioral norms and language, these skills and their practice within the framework of the assumptions and principles are the core of a leadership culture. How people work with each other day-to-day expresses a company's culture.

- Curiosity: A genuine interest in understanding another person's perspective, thinking, and learning.
- Level 2 and 3 Listening: Putting attention on the other person and listening with curiosity is Level 2 listening. Doing so enables the listener to hear what is important to the other, what they want, etc. Level 3 adds the listener's intuition and the speaker's mood and non-verbal responses.
- Powerful Questions: Open-ended questions that stimulate reflection, discovery, and clarity. They lead to awareness and action.

- Coaching Roadmap: A process that emphasizes defining a clear vision and a plan to create the desired outcome and minimizing attention on the perceived limitations imposed by the current circumstances.
- Accountability: A promise to take a specific action by a certain time and to communicate the result.
- Acknowledgement: Speaking to a person's character in the pursuit of a goal. It does not require the successful completion of the goal.

Using these skills is a commitment to learning and growing as a leader. Within a leadership culture people view themselves and everyone else as a leader. They realize that theirs and everyone else's success depends on continuing to learn. So, they demand of each other support for their learning and using these skills with each other, accomplish learning from every challenge and situation encountered at work.

## The Road to Success

Building a leadership culture is a personal growth process. It begins with working with beliefs, attitudes, aspirations— the heart of each person. Leadership cannot be delegated; it begins and ends with each employee, regardless of job title. This chapter began by describing successful companies as those with the courage to delve into the internal workings of humans. Managers who have the discipline to reflect on their attitudes, assumptions, and aspirations; the courage to receive feedback; and who reveal and work with what is in their hearts, will guide companies living a leadership culture. There is no program or consultant to be purchased that relieves a leader from this responsibility.

Kevin Cashman highlights the spiritual nature of the inside-out change needed: "As much as we try to separate the leader from the person, the two are totally inseparable...Leadership is not simply something we do. It comes from somewhere inside us. Leadership is a process, an intimate expression of who we are. It is our being in action."[10] And, this is a practice. Outside-in programs have a specific beginning and end. Personal growth has no specific end point; the learning is on-going.

Growing a leadership culture is a top-down process. It begins at the executive level. This is a simple, yet more difficult change. Simpler because lower levels come into alignment with behavior they experience daily. More difficult because it calls forth executives to reveal their authentic selves, which includes successes and failures, strengths and weaknesses. Attempts at middle-out or bottom-up change produce limited results that fade with time. However, when executives make the personal commitment, the change will be long lasting and effective.

The first phase of building a leadership culture includes the following basic elements.

1. **Individual Executive Coaching.** Initially, the executive gets clear about his or her personal mission, vision, and values and how to bring those to the job, setting goals and plans. Later the coach supports the executive in achieving those goals and in the on-going practice of their leadership.

2. **Executive Team Coaching.** The executive team designs their version of a leadership culture. The coach guides the design and supports the team in the practice of working together according to the design.

3. **Skills Training for the Executives.** Executives learn the leadership culture skills and how to apply them daily.

4. **Roll out to next management layer.** The basic steps are repeated at the Director level with shorter individual coaching time and adaptation of the training to the specific needs of this group. The team coaching may not be included, depending on the organization.

5. **Roll out to middle management and individual contributors.** The specifics vary widely according to the size of the company, its geographical distribution, and the speed of the roll out. There is usually training for each level. The individual coaching occurs primarily within the existing work relationships.

This list looks similar to any training program. The difference is the deep personal growth and individual attention each person experiences. This high level of personal involvement delivers immediate impact. Change begins with the first coaching conversation. All-hands meetings, project management teams, and banners are not required, or even desired, for the shift to a leadership culture. The change to a leadership culture comes down to each executive committing to working together as leaders, with each one being authentic, creating value in every interaction, and taking responsibility for their impact.

This is not another "movement" or fad requiring wholesale organizational change. It is simply—and profoundly—people choosing to work together in a heartfelt, human-to-human way that delivers astounding business performance.

**References:**

1. Bennis, Warren, and Joan Goldsmith. *Learning To Lead: A Workbook On Becoming A Leader*, Cambridge, MA: Perseus Books, 1997, page XV.

2. Bennis, Warren, and Joan Goldsmith. *Learning To Lead: A Workbook On Becoming A Leader*, Cambridge, MA: Perseus Books, 1997, page XV.

3. Buckingham, Marcus and Curt Coffman. *First, Break All The Rules: What The World's Greatest Managers Do Differently*, New York: Simon and Schuster, NY, 1999.

4. Cashman, Kevin . *Leadership From The Inside Out: Becoming a Leader for Life*, Utah: Executive Excellence Publishing, Provo, 1998, page 20.

5. Deal, Terrence E., and Allan A. Kennedy. *Corporate Cultures: The Rites And Rituals Of Corporate Life,* Cambridge, MA: Perseus Books, 2000.

6. Kimsey-House, Henry, Phil Sandahl and Laura Whitworth. *Co-Active Coaching: New Skills for Coaching People Toward Success in Work and Life,* Palo Alto: Davies-Black Publishing, 1998, page 3.

7. Probst, Gilbert J.B. *Organizational Learning: The Competitive Advantage of the Future,* Prentice Hall, 1997.

8. LaBarre, Polly. Interview with Peter Koestenbaum, *Do You Have the Will to Lead?,* Fast Company magazine, Issue 32, March 2000, page 222.

9. Kimsey-House, Henry, Phil Sandahl and Laura Whitworth. *Co-Active Coaching: New Skills for Coaching People Toward Success in Work and Life,* Palo Alto: Davies-Black Publishing, 1998.

10. Cashman, Kevin. *Leadership From The Inside Out: Becoming a Leader for Life,* Provo, Utah: Executive Excellence Publishing, 1998.

11. Collins, Jim. *Good To Great: Why Some Companies Make the Leap…and Others Don't,* New York: HarperCollins, 2001.

## About
## Innerworks Solutins

Innerworks Solutions is a leadership development company that works with organizations to build a "Leadership Culture." They believe that everyone is a leader 100% of the time and that each individual can co-actively create value every day in every interaction. Innerworks Solutions offers simple yet profound ways for people to interact with each other at work, so that the work experience can be more meaningful and rewarding.

With a management team of three founders, plus a prestigious group of outside independent contractors, Innerworks Solutions' reach spans the United States, Canada, and Europe. Innerworks Solutions' customers range from small and medium size business to divisions of Fortune 500 multinational companies. They maintain an excellent reputation for providing high quality and productive programs at value-based pricing.

**Mai Vu, CPCC, MA**, is a co-founder and Co-CEO of Innerworks Solutions. A boat person from Vietnam, she brings 6 + years of corporate and over six years of coaching experience. Mai's extensive background includes participation on the Board of the International Coaching Federation (ICF) and trainer, supervisor, and certification examiner with the Coaches Training Institute (CTI). A former mechanical engineer, she has a passion to bring out the leader in people at work, where they can be alive, creative, and authentic.

**Shariann Tom, CPCC,** is a co-founder and Co-CEO of Innerworks Solutions. A two-time cancer survivor, she brings 16 years of corporate and four years of coaching experience. Shariann's background includes participation on the Business Council for UC Berkeley's SAGE Scholar Program and a leader of workshops for cancer survivors. A former Sales and Marketing manager, she advocates that people are both key resources and the heart of a company.

**John Vercelli, MCC, CPCC, MA**, is a co-founder and Co-CEO of Innerworks Solutions. A Stanford graduate, John's background also includes his role as a senior leader for CTI, where he trains coaches and leaders to realize their full potential. A former electrical engineer and business manager, he draws on 17 years of corporate and 10 years of coaching experience to bring alive his leadership work in organizations.

# CULTURE-vating

## By Duane Reed

The manager looks out of his office toward the break area, eyebrows twisted in anger. He notices four employees, including his hand-picked assistant, standing there talking! "What the?" he says, as he jerks out of his chair and walks briskly toward the group that is violating his rules on taking breaks. He walks up to the four and says sternly, "Get back to work," and keeps on walking. The four glance at one another, and the assistant manager starts to speak again. Since the group did not disperse immediately, the manager looks back over his shoulder and shouts, "NOW!" Each member of the group heads back to his desk and the manager arrogantly thinks, "Mission accomplished."

Embarrassingly, I admit that I was that manager. Are you wondering what happened next? Well, I called the assistant manager into my office with the intention of making him an example of what happens to someone breaking one of "my rules." He explained that he had asked the other three to join him to plan for a client audit that would take place later in the day. He also reminded me that I had promised him the prior week that I would have such a meeting by yesterday, but the meeting never happened. Concerned about our lack of preparation for the client audit, the assistant was getting the input needed for the audit when I "went off."

The year was 1983, and though I was only twenty-something, I had seven years of experience as a manager. Well, really, I had one year of experience times seven, as I had not yet learned how best to influence my team of nearly sixty men and women. I was still resorting to using my position and authority to dictate the actions of others.

As bad as I looked in that scenario, there were other things in terms of managerial leadership that were just as inappropriate, such as not following through on promises, inconsistency, insensitivity of all kinds, and showing favoritism. In terms of creating a culture conducive for maximum long-term productivity, I was failing.

Unfortunately, this behavior is not extinct! Even now, in the twenty-first century, poor management leading to lack of leadership and nearly toxic work cultures is one of the major complaints I hear from employees. The size of the company has very little to do with poor management. I have heard this complaint from employees of Fortune 50 companies to entrepreneurial ventures with a handful of workers. One of the goals of my life's work is to assist managers and business owners in making the transformations necessary to make extinct the type of dictatorial, self-serving, mean-spirited, or unconscious behavior that I was guilty of in the example above. These transformations lead the way to developing skills that enable managers to create cultures that support, encourage, and reward all employees, cultures that are conducive to the highest possible employee productivity.

## The 6 C's

> "IN LIFE, YOU GET WHAT YOU GIVE."
> ~ ANONYMOUS

There are hundreds of factors involved in managerial success: timing, location, financial backing, new technologies, the state of the world economy, supportive partners, and board members, to name a few. As individual managers, we don't have much control over most of these. But there are components of management over which we *do* have control. I call them the "6 C's." In the following pages I will present thumbnail descriptions of each these six components.

I once heard someone say that, "Every mundane effort brings forth ripples of growth." A simple change in the way we interact with an employee *can* have an enormous impact on that person's attitude. And one employee's attitude can affect many other employees. Thus, the whole company culture is impacted. My company's name is Inside Success because I believe inside is where success starts: inside ourselves *and* inside our company. So, as you read this, ask yourself how your interactions have been impacting the culture of your team, department, company, or corporation. Are you getting the kind of results you really want? What can you change on the inside that would improve the quality of your group's culture and work life for you and those around you? Consider one or more of the Six C's as development areas.

### The First "C" of Remarkable Culture-vating Skills: Consciousness

*"CONSCIOUSNESS: THE ACT OF BECOMING AWARE THAT WHAT ONE SAYS AND DOES IMPACTS WHAT OTHERS SAY AND DO."*

*~ DUANE REED*

When facilitating management training workshops, I often ask participants to identify as many dualities as they can. For example, up/down, good/evil, hot/cold, off/on, and slow/fast. Then, I offer one more: conscious and unconscious. Most of the group will knowingly chuckle and laugh. I then do a fifteen-second consciousness test with the group in which ninety-seven to one hundred percent of the participants fail. I now have the managers' attention and with very little help from me, they brainstorm *why* they were "unconscious" for the exercise. Next, I instruct them to make analogies to their work. Some will say they failed the test because of an incorrect expectation. I ask, "How many of you have ever expected employees to do certain things that they did not do?" Everyone raises their hand.

Another reason I often hear why managers fail the test is that I give them only fifteen seconds to complete it and they feel "rushed." I'll ask the group, "How many of you ever feel rushed here at _____ Company?" Now they really laugh and again the hands go up. Maybe you've experienced the more work with fewer people and resources trend. This trend of companies "doing more with less" is probably not going to change. What do you lose when you feel rushed? Attention to detail and focus? The ability to communicate properly with your employees? Managers are especially susceptible to this type of unconsciousness because of the very nature of their jobs. They are the purveyors of information.

Information. Managers are typically tasked with the responsibility of juggling tremendous amounts of it: internal and external customer information, upper management's wishes, product knowledge, compliance and regulatory information, goals, deadlines, fires to put out, employee questions to answer, training's to facilitate. The list is endless. By the time a manager gets to a genuine employee management opportunity such as providing feedback to an employee or informing the team that a procedural change is about to be implemented, she doesn't take the time to determine the best way to package the information, she just does it. It can be brutal. Remember the opening example depicting how I interacted with the four employees? It's not that I didn't know how to better interact with them. I just believed I was too busy, perhaps too important to worry about how those people may have felt. I was certainly too unconscious to care about how they felt. Having grown in consciousness, I would handle the situation quite differently today. I would not just jump to the conclusion that the group was goofing off. I would be prepared to be empathetic, show sincerity, and ask questions. Like, "Hi folks. Another busy day huh? Do you need any input or help from me?" Imagine the busiest of days. In the middle of it, you have an opportunity to provide feedback for improvement to an employee. If you are not prepared, the wrong words might come out. Think of some of the ways you have handled this in the past. Can you identify any inappropriate actions? What would you do differently?

### The Inevitabilities

There is a book titled *Work Would Be Great If It Weren't For The People*. I believe this theory applies to management, as well. My wife Kathryn would certainly agree. She worked for two years as the Customer Service Manager for a mid-sized company. Every night she would come home and unload. Quibbling between employees; irrational and even neurotic behaviors of the owner; the impatient, overly demanding, and sometimes mean-spirited customers. Did I say every night? *Every single night* I heard variations on the same stories. Of course, I always tried to listen intently and be supportive. One night, while listening to yet another story punctuated with colorful expletives, I had one of my better moments of consciousness. "Honey, what will happen tomorrow?" I began. "I mean, what will inevitably occur tomorrow?" After some discussion, she "discovered" that her job had *certain inherent and difficult inevitabilities*. There were things that were inevitably going to happen. As managers, when we consciously recognize what will inevitably occur in our day, we can better prepare mentally and emotionally to deal with it appropriately.

Recently, I was training managers in a California office of a large national telecommunications company. It was 8:30 am. Just as I was to begin the training, I realized that one of the attendees was very upset. She was telling another manager that two of her ten direct reports had come in late. She went on and on about how every day someone from her department comes in late, often citing traffic problems. "We live in Los Angeles, for God's sake, and they're surprised there's traffic!" During most of my morning training, it was obvious to me that this manager was distracted by thoughts of the chronic lateness of her employees. To the manager's credit, in one of the exercises she "owned" the distraction and came to realize that it is inevitable someone will be late to work. Now, she can consciously determine the best way to handle this situation and the proper versus improper behavior response. Best, in this instance, would be defined as the consciously mature, professional, rational way.

What distracting negative inevitabilities does your job have? Think about these inevitabilities. If you *accepted* that each day certain inevitabilities were going to occur, would you act, react, or interact differently? By becoming more conscious of these inevitabilities, one can cope by adjusting behaviors and actions accordingly. You may be asking, "What's in it for me?" For one thing, you'll be less like I was back in '83!

## The Second "C" of Remarkable Culture-vating Skills: Communication

"COMMUNICATION: THE ART OF EXPOSING OTHERS TO HOW WE ARE FEELING ABOUT THEM, THE COMPANY, AND OURSELVES."

~ DUANE REED

Communication is the single most important skill a manager should have. More corporate training sessions have been conducted on communication than any other subject. Why? Because good communication can be very complicated. There are so many factors: voice inflection, pacing, timing, articulation, pitch, tone, and volume. Even when we're not talking, we're talking! We are communicating with facial expressions, breathing patterns, body language, and even silence. Communication has often been referred to as an art, and the better skilled a manager is in this art, the more likely it is his people will be optimally productive and issues such as poor performance, poor work habits, and employee retention will diminish. If you feel you are lacking effective communication skills, I encourage you to work with a communication coach or do self-study on the topic and practice in front of a mirror.

This section could have been titled "the motive of communication," as it has been said that, "Communication is depositing part of yourself in another person." This can be both a calming thought and a very scary thought. Imagine having a manager who is dictatorial and self-centered and treats you like a lowly subordinate. Now picture another manager, one who uses positive words to influence you, is "others"-centered, and treats you in a manner that confirms you are valuable to the company. How do their motives differ? How would they communicate with you differently? Which one would you rather work for? Be more loyal to? Which one is creating the kind of *culture* in which you would prefer to work? Companies are dedicating larger portions of their training budgets to training manager's certain soft skills. Soft skills include ways to boost or maintain self-esteem; being an empathetic listener and leader; knowing when and how to ask for support and motivate others to provide support to co-workers or a company goal; and even how to verbalize the emotions, opinions, and thought processes behind decisions that affect the work force.

Twenty years ago, a friend possessing exceptional writing skills was told by the managing editor of an upscale magazine that her writing wasn't very good. His communication ("red ink that flowed like a river of blood," to quote my friend) impacted her so greatly that while she still wrote, she shared her writing only with the trusted people closest to her. Now, finally, she is putting her work out there, and it is being praised and accepted for publication. What was the editor's motive? Suppose my friend had considered that the reason the editor painted her work in red was because he was jealous of her talent. She would have kept on writing and submitting her work and, instead of being a budding author, she would now have twenty years of experience.

Think about some of the managers you have had. Include your parents, as they were our first managers. Now, imagine you had the power to visualize the actual motives of positive and negative communications you received from these managers. How have the various communications affected you and your life? Think about the type of manager you have been. Have you ever negatively affected someone who was undeserving? Managers can improve their company's culture by understanding the art of communication and their own motives. What message do you want to send to your employees?

## The Third "C" of Remarkable Culture-vating Skills: Creativity

> "CREATIVITY: THE ACT OF INJECTING FUN AND POSITIVE VARIATIONS INTO EVERYDAY MUNDANE ACTIVITIES."
>
> ~ DUANE REED

Dread. Pure dread. Sandy felt it swelling up within her as she reached to hit the snooze alarm for the third time. The feeling swirled into thoughts of her mother saying, "When you snooze, you lose." And then guilt, that evil sister of dread, appeared. "It's Friday," she mumbled, settling back into her down pillow. "I should be happy to go to work! But all I feel is dread. Doing the same job over and over, day in and day out. The only variation is training a new person who replaced another new person. The turnover is so high, it's hard to keep track of all the people coming and going. It wasn't always like this. What happened?"

Every job is fun the first day! But what about at the end of six months? A year? A decade!? Many tangible factors can affect the workplace culture, from the color of the walls to the height of the cubicles to the lighting to the type of chairs to the location of the vending machines to the type of flooring and on and on. But what about the *intangible* factors? They are as crucial in maintaining a positive work culture as the tangible factors.

Every manager of people is in charge of these intangible factors. The knowing ones "work" at creatively injecting variation into the mundane. They seize opportunities to do something different. Perhaps it's making a big deal about naming a new product. Or welcoming a new client with great fanfare. Maybe it is simply getting a better copier or phone system and they take turns bashing the old one with a sledge-hammer. Perhaps it is hosting a monthly covered-dish lunch or coming up with a productivity-related contest. Perhaps it's getting a vendor to host a lunch or an after-hours party. What about pizza day? Creativity has no limits or boundaries.

One of the most creative things managers can do is empower their people to come up with something they think will be fun or entertaining. The manager just makes it "okay" to have fun periodically. It doesn't have to be grandiose. Sometimes simple is better. Give employees something to look forward to, something that makes going to work less dreadful, routine, and uneventful. Human beings are, after-all, *creative* beings. Be sure to attend the events; it's important that the manager shows support.

Creativity is, of course, not just event-oriented. In our day-to-day interactions, there are many opportunities to be creative. Ask other managers how they create a culture where people want to come to work. List some of the ways you could bring more creativity to your workplace. Use the brainstorming method, ignoring for the moment cost, practicality, and appropriateness. Thinking positive, creative thoughts is contagious. Imagine the possibilities.

## The Fourth "C" of Remarkable Culture-vating Skills: Courtesy

*"COURTESY: ACT TO EXCEED EXPECTATIONS."*

*~ DUANE REED*

BeepHonk! BeepHonk! The irritating sounds of his own car horn only makes Jeremy feel angrier. But he continues. BeepHonk! Beephonk! He's in a hurry. First day on a new job and he's late. In front of him is a semi-truck in the right lane and some jack_ _ _ in a Cadillac in the left passing lane who is just keeping pace with the big hauler. Jeremy is behind the Cadillac flashing his lights and honking. This has been going on for about five miles, and Jeremy is about to lose it. Literally. The Cadillac finally speeds up allowing just enough gap for Jeremy to snake through. He jerks his car in front of the truck and as he passes the Cadillac he flips the guy off with the appropriate finger. The distinguished man just smiles back at him.

Upon arrival at his new office, Angie from Human Resources, Jeremy's contact for orientation greets him. She asks Jeremy to have a seat while she gets some paperwork for him. Looking around, Jeremy is struck by the calm intensity and the focused blur of interaction between employees. "This is different," he thinks to himself, "What is it?" As he watches, he begins to pick up on a rhythm. The people are, well, courteous and even nice to one another. "This is definitely different than the job I just left," he thinks to himself.

In fact, it was the overall rudeness of people that drove him away from his middle management position. He found himself becoming one of them. Rude, gossipy, distrusting, even lying to "get ahead." But, it was not who he really wanted to be. Jeremy knew he wanted to be trusted and respected, not feared and talked about negatively. Angie returned with a questionnaire unlike any Jeremy has seen. "The boss, and the department heads read every questionnaire," she stated proudly.

Jeremy's heart raced as he read the questions. What are your strengths? What are some of your areas of development? Do you like to receive feedback in writing, over the phone, e-mail, or in person? How do you feel about interruptions? Do you prefer I drop in or make an appointment? When you're not in your cubicle or office, and I have something for you, should I put it in an in-box, on your chair, or on your desk? In total, there were 20 questions all pertaining to how Jeremy wanted others to interact with him!

Jeremy takes the completed questionnaire to Angie. "Are you ready to meet the CEO?" she asks. Jeremy follows Angie's lead. "There he is." She points toward the end of the long corridor. Jeremy strains to get a better look. The man looks familiar. Too familiar. Jeremy feels his stomach sink and the floor beneath him give way. "Oh my God. It's the Cadillac man."

Courtesy. There is a time and place for it: **always and everywhere.** And it can take many forms: opening a door for someone, promptly returning a phone call, providing support to others, communicating fully with others, even when the message is unpopular or controversial, offering reasons for changes, and on and on. What can you do to be more courteous? Remember, you don't own the road.

## The Fifth "C" of Remarkable Culture-vating Skills: Consistency

*"CONSISTENCY: THE ACT OF LETTING GO OF THE JUSTIFICATIONS AND RATIONALIZATIONS THAT REINFORCE OUR MANAGERIAL MEDIOCRITY."*

*~ DUANE REED*

On a Monday morning at 7 a.m., I watch as a man pulls up to the curb in his sleek European luxury sedan. You know, the one that starts with the letter J. Giant raindrops shoot like bullets off the recently waxed silver hood. He gets out anyway, turns, and stoops to retrieve something from the passenger seat. The rain soaks his dark gray Armani suit. Deliberately, the man pulls from the car a rather large item, closes the car door, and walks up the steps to the building's front door.

I continue to watch, standing at the doorway waiting, mostly sheltered from the blowing rain as the well-aged man hustles up the steps with a grin on his face. He is carrying a box filled with still-warm bagels, various spreads, fresh fruit, and juice. The distinguished gentleman lugging the box full of snacks is David L., the owner of a very successful company that has hired me to conduct a series of ninety-minute presentations on various topics. Today's is effective customer service. I find it surprising that he hasn't delegated this responsibility and ask why he has done the shopping, which required at least two stops. "My assistant is running late," he begins, "and it is important I meet the expectations of the crew," referring to his team of about thirty employees.

I was very impressed. His crew would have understood not having the snacks this one time. They knew his schedule put him in the office usually at nine, not seven, and then there is this horrible weather. But, being a man of integrity, David went the extra mile, literally, to fulfill what he believed was an obligation. He could have easily used the early hour and inclement weather to justify skipping the treats. Of course, since the training topic of the day was customer service, this act of the owner struck me as a customer service highlight. His employees are his internal customers, and he certainly provided them with exceptional service. This story is an excellent example of the role consistency plays in the lives of those who manage and those who are managed.

Remarkable managers strive to have consistent behaviors, attitudes, decision-making processes, actions, reactions, and interactions. They consistently do ordinary things extraordinarily well. They consistently go beyond what's expected, add value and integrity to every interaction, and discover new ways to be effective with those they lead and serve. Managers who have developed consistency in their leadership know good leadership is an all-day attitude, not an afterthought: "I should've, I could've, oh well, whatever!" Consistency in management means taking care of employees as if the successes of the manager's life and career depend on it. Remarkable managers consistently walk the talk.

Okay. I know. No one is always that remarkable. But you are reading this book aren't you? So, one can be consistent in pursuing consistency, and that means gaining consciousness around what needs to be improved. Pick one thing to improve. Pick another that you do well and pat yourself on the back.

### The Sixth "C" of Remarkable Culture-vating Skills: Commitment

*"COMMITMENT: WHAT YOU DO EVEN WHEN YOU DON'T FEEL LIKE IT. IT'S WHAT GETS YOU THROUGH THE HARD TIMES. COMMITMENT IS REMEMBERING WHAT IT IS YOU WANT AND TAKING APPROPRIATE ACTION TO GET IT."*

*~ DUANE REED*

Do you like movies? What about a movie of you at work? With the camera following you around every day, for twelve weeks. And at the end of each week, the movie is televised on HBO. That's what happened to Chris Moore, the executive producer for the 2002 movie "Stolen Summer." HBO's behind-the-scenes camera followed Mr. Moore and captured on film his interactions with the film crew, especially first-time screen writer and director, Pete Jones. Mr. Moore, in an interview on Oprah, said, "I wish I'd handled myself differently. Intimidating people and screaming at people is not necessarily the best way to motivate people or to get their best work. It did not help anything." I don't know Mr. Moore, but I do know that seeing one's self in a "less than perfect" light can have quite a profound effect. But, without commitment, his demeanor and management style will not change. And so, you may be wondering, "How do I become more committed?"

One idea is to make a list of all the personal characteristics you dislike about yourself. Write these characteristics in a column, then write the opposite characteristic next to it. Examples would be: Arrogant/Humble, Vague/Determinate, Judgmental/Open-minded. Carry the page with you. Whenever you find yourself acting out a negative characteristic, look at the list, then convey the opposite characteristic. This really worked for me. I wrote my first list in 1994. There were over thirty negative characteristics on the page. I carried it for about two years. I admit I still act out some of them, but not nearly as often or as intensely. One of my favorite phrases is, "Willingness without action is fantasy; don't confuse motion with action." This exercise helped me put into action my desire to change. Look at the quote that opened this component. Sometimes you won't feel like changing, but when you do, that is being committed. Being committed is when you remember what you really want. Be committed.

Most of us will never be filmed like Mr. Moore. But, what if you were? What commitment would you make each day you go to work? What would you change if you committed to manage every moment of every day like you were being filmed? What characteristics would you let go of and what would you replace them with? Improving the culture of your team, department, company or corporation starts with improving you.

### In Conclusion

As the person in charge, you determine the culture within the team, department, company, or corporation. The six "C's" can be your guide to taking that culture to the next level. Be the catalyst of cultural growth and change. Be a remarkable manager rather than just the person with the title of manager. Be one who leads his people to create a new culture with new beliefs and behaviors. And don't just be *willing* to grow and change, because, *willingness without action is fantasy*. And don't be like some people and confuse motion with action. Take action! Be committed. Communicate courteously your commitment to CULTURE-vating a consistent creative consciousness! And you *will be* a great success!!

### About
### Duane Reed

Indiana born and raised, Duane Reed has been using his listening and leadership gifts since childhood. From setting the emotional tone in his kindergarten class to achieving the honor of being the youngest Eagle Scout in Indiana to managing over 60 employees, Duane's skills have resulted in drawing 7500+ audiences to his training, coaching, and consulting company during the past twenty years. "I will train any soft skill to anyone, anywhere, anytime, and exceed expectations" is the slogan of his company, Inside Success™. And he has the experience to support such a statement.

After a decade of counseling crime survivors and victims' families and helping people create (and re-create) fulfilling lives, Duane found continued success in helping individuals, companies, corporations, and government entities get from where they are to where they want to be by creating the internal culture necessary to attain goal achievement. Training to over 300 industries has helped him excel where other trainers have failed. His depth of knowledge, understanding, optimism, and humor, combined with endless energy has shaped him into a flexible and adaptive presenter, trainer, and coach.

In 1990, Duane began writing and conducting self-development workshops, his most popular being *The LifeBalance Workshop©*. This workshop incorporates his *Empowerment Exercise©*, which helps people determine where they have been, where they are, and where they want to be in all categories of life. This consciousness sparks the pro-active focusing of energy in one to three categories and indirect energy toward the rest. Graduates accomplished tasks and goals they believed were beyond their capabilities and achieved balance in their lives. "Those who follow the steps of my *Inside Success Goal Achievement Program©* and use *The Accountability Factor©* always achieve their goals."

Duane's talent as a speaker, communicator, trainer, facilitator, and humorist shines when he is addressing executives, managers, sales people, customer service representatives, and individual contributors. To meet the needs of these various groups, Inside Success offers an extensive menu of topics ranging from leadership development and team-building to sales and customer service. Areas addressed within these topics include interpersonal skills, flexibility in managing/leading, adapting to change, making decisions more effectively, preventing the underachieving of teams and individuals, telephone and e-mail etiquette, The Art of Leading by Asking the Right Questions the Right Way©, The Customer's Bill of Rights©, and much more.

According to Duane, "Willingness without action is fantasy; don't confuse motion with action!"

If you are not getting the results you want in your life or your work, please contact Duane in Denver, Colorado at (720) 373-3777 or DuaneReed@InsideSuccess.net. For more information, visit his website at www.InsideSucces.net.

# Becoming a Remarkable Manager

## By Chuck Schultz

What makes a remarkable manager? If you look at those amazing managers that you have worked with in the past, what would you say are their best talents?

- Is it the ability to communicate effectively?
- Is it compassion for those they manage?
- Is it holding high standards for themselves as well as those they work with?
- Is it seeing others as greater than they see themselves?

You may be saying, "Any one of those things!" However, will any one of these things really create a remarkable manager? Or, will any **one** of these create merely a good manager? In my opinion, a really great manager has all of the skills listed above, and more.

What is essential for truly remarkable managers is the ability to see an organization as more than just parts or a sum of parts. To illustrate, let me present a model of five elements that has worked well in organizations I have coached. At the base is Certainty, the next level up is Significance, then Team/Connection, followed by Values/Shared Vision, and at the top, Strategic Thinking/Results Focus. In this chapter, I will describe each of the elements, and how to implement them in an organization.

## Certainty

Everyone has a need to feel certain that their environment is stable at some level. Even in the high technology fields where it appears that people thrive on chaos, there is a need for Certainty. Different levels of Certainty obviously apply. People want to feel certain that they will have a job tomorrow; that they will be able to cash their paycheck; that what upper management tells them is the truth. What are some things that have caused you to feel uncertain in jobs in the past? A manager who does not support his team? Ongoing restructuring? I have a client who in the last seven years at a large corporation has been through six restructures. You have to wonder what kind of Certainty, if any, that client might have.

Let me give you an example of a company I worked with that was in trouble. Their turnover was high and they had lost 30% of their business to competition. They had become financially strapped because of not being prepared for an economic downturn and not anticipating the need to update with new developments in technology. When we talked with the current employees, the big question on everyone's mind was, "Will I have a job next week, month, or year?" With that as an underlying theme in the day-to-day operations, how effective do you feel the company was? The company was busy watching cash flow and was not paying attention to what the employees needed.

Here is what we did to help get the company back on track. There were several long-term employees in the company that were in need of acknowledgement for their loyalty. We began by implementing an employee recognition program. Each of these employees was openly thanked for what they had done for the company. Next, those employees that had been with the company for more than three years were brought into a meeting as representatives for their specific area. Under confidentiality, the status of the company was discussed. Ideas were solicited from the employees and here's the big action that was taken: the ideas were implemented. When asked later about that meeting and the subsequent actions, the employees said that they felt more like they were in control of the business. The meeting gave them a sense of certainty that they were heard and that their opinions mattered. As a result, not only are those employees still with the company, the company has rebounded. As a result of these changes, employee turnover has dropped to almost zero and the company has returned to profitability. The entrepreneur who runs the company has less stress in his life and can spend more time with his family. All in all, a very successful turnaround.

### Significance

Let me ask you this. How does it feel if someone says to you, "I really want to recognize how you worked on that project. If it were not for you I don't know if we would have met our goal."? Say that to yourself and see how it feels. (Did you say it to yourself?) If you did you probably felt a feeling of importance—a feeling like you had Significance in the world. We all have a need to feel this in our lives and especially in the work place. People must feel that they are important to the operation of the organization. This goes for everyone. It doesn't matter if someone is in a bookkeeping position, on a production line, in management, in engineering, in sales, or in shipping. *Everyone* has a need to feel significant, like they matter to the world.

Can someone feel Significant if they do not have Certainty in the organization or their position in the organization? Ask yourself another question. If you had a manager that walked up to you and said, "I really appreciate the way you handled that account, you really are a top performer. It is because of you that we kept them as a client. Oh, and could you do me a favor? Would you wait until Monday to cash your check, I am not sure if we have the funds to cover payroll until then?"

Would you feel less certain about the company? Less certain about your manager's reasons for complimenting you so highly, no matter how well deserved? Would you feel significant at all? Or would you feel like the only reason for the compliment was to get an accommodation from you?

If you or your division, department, company, or business unit does not have the Certainty that they will have a job, get a paycheck, be heard, that the company does what it says it will do, will never feel a level of Significance.

Now that you have established a level of Certainty, how do you establish a level of Significance? A sincere and specific compliment goes a long way. What would you consider a sincere and specific compliment for you? It needs to be a direct and timely recognition for a job well done. This recognition must also be specific.

Let's say that Jane has just pulled in a new client, which is her job. A great response would be; "Jane, do you have a minute? I wanted to thank you for landing that new contract with ABC, Inc. I really appreciate the amount of effort that you put in. I know you spent some long hours on it and they had some specific needs. Thank you for putting in the great effort."

There is a key element of giving this kind of compliment to someone. It is *very important* that this is done in the open. If someone gets a compliment behind closed doors, it is as if it never happened. However, just as it is vital to boost someone's Significance by complimenting them in public, it is equally important to remember to give constructive feedback in private. Nothing will tear away this feeling of Significance more than criticizing them in public. Even a comment of, "Johnson, can I talk to you in my office, *now!*" diminishes one's feeling of Significance. The more private the constructive feedback is, the better it will be received. And remember, if the only time you "close the door to your office" is when you are criticizing someone, guess what? Everybody knows that! It would be as if it were done in public. If you ask someone into your office to give them a sincere compliment and you close the door, now nobody else knows exactly what's been said and the rumors start flying.

### Team/Connection

So we have Certainty and we have Significance. Now we can start working on true Team. Here, we want to develop a sense of Connection with those in the office that allows everyone to flourish. A true team is one that supports each other, they share information freely, and are always looking for ways they can help one another. This can be characterized by the phrase, "Your needs are my needs." Most things that we accomplish we do through teams, whether we are a sole proprietorship or part of a large multinational company. To see the team from the entrepreneur's vantage point, we would look at who helps them do business. Among these can be their Lawyer, Accountant, Marketing Media, Printer, Banker, Vendors, and, of course, their Customers. In a large organization, the Team may be a business unit, a work unit, a division, or department.

We have all heard so much about Team development. There are several theories and ways to develop Teams. And usually what we run into are dysfunctional teams. I believe that the reason for this is that the first two levels—Certainty and Significance—are not satisfied. I work with teams regularly for experiential learning. What I see across the board is that those teams whose members have Certainty and Significance perform at a much higher level. One of the key points that I work with in this environment is getting team members to support and encourage at the levels that allow the team to truly function.

I recently worked with a group from a large pharmaceutical company. The division had a wide mix of people. Approximately 50% of the group obviously lacked Certainty. They did not know why they were at the program, were not sure of the department due to recent downsizing, and they questioned if they were being evaluated that day for job performance. All of these questions destroyed any feeling of Certainty. Of the remainder of the group, most were trying to gain Significance by making a joke of things, attempting to take charge and telling people what to do, not agreeing with others because their ideas were not being used. Those that did have Certainty and Significance did not sit back and wait for others to "get it." They were willing to work on the team and made attempts to give Certainty and

Significance to others. It appeared that, consciously or not, they knew what the others needed.

I also worked with a group of High School students that already had high levels of Certainty and because of the program that they were in, they had a high level of Significance. On the other hand, most of the High School counselors who were participating lacked Certainty. A comment from one counselor was, "If I fall off once, I quit!" The students performed at such a high level that they completed elements in record time. One activity that normally takes an hour or more, they completed in 15 minutes. We played one game that split the group into three smaller groups. I intentionally set the counselors out from the students, so they appeared to be pitted against the students. Less then three minutes into the activity, the counselors were in overwhelm and frustrated. They felt they could not "win" and gave up. I was shocked. The students kept working, kept problem solving, and when they came up with a solution where everyone would win, the counselors were skeptical that this was a valid solution and chose not to participate again. This to me was a stark example of how true teamwork can happen as long as there is Certainty and Significance. And how it doesn't happen when those elements are lacking.

The question then becomes, "How do we foster true teamwork?" In reality there can only be one answer: create an environment where people feel Certain and are rewarded with a feeling of Significance and your team will start to develop naturally. What are some things that help to bring a team together? A common enemy is a great way to do that. By a common enemy I don't suggest that you become the overbearing team leader or that the company become adversarial to employees. The "enemy" could be a competitor that has come up with a product or service that is seen as a threat. Or, it could be "The Big Client" that everybody wants to land. There are times during a team event that I will play the "bad cop" role to create a common enemy. However, as a team leader I would not suggest that tactic.

### Values/Shared Vision

A very important component for any team to have is shared Values. Values are things you do or that you find very attractive, that provide an emotional state that you strive for. When engaged in these activities or feeling these emotions, you feel most like your true self. You are well, healthy, and complete. You feel connected and are excited about life. People may say that you glow; there is an "energy" about you. In a lot of ways things become effortless. Values are things that we want and like to have in our lives, yet most of us lead lives in which we do not allow the space to just do these things, or let ourselves feel these feelings. Many of us spend our lives trying (consciously or not) to experience these values.

Everyone has values and even rules on how they are met. When our values are in conflict with someone else there will likely be conflict between us. In an organization, having similar values will be critical for growth. In an organization, we will always have people whose values are not in alignment with our own. As a great leader there are two things that we can do. We can foster those values that are in common to help others reflect the values back toward each other. The other is to help those that we are leading to recognize and embrace the differences in values and understand, learn, and use communication tools with each other.

One way to determine values is to take an assessment that will help people discover the values most important to them. Two assessments that I have used in the past are the DISC model and the OAD model. Each has great information and can be applied to an entire team.

Another way to elicit values is to use a guided process of questions that will help someone determine their own values. Questions like, "What emotion is it most important for me to feel in Business (or in this team)?" You can do this for any personal situation as well. If you use Life instead of Business you will get your highest values in Life. The same applies to Relationships. All you need to do is ask yourself this question or use a coach to guide you and your team through the process. You may also want to prioritize the list by asking the question, "Is it more important for me to feel _____ or _____?" This will give you your list of values from most important to less important.

Why are we here? Now, that is a universal question. If we ask this question of the people in an organization, we will likely hear a number of views of why the organization exists. How would it feel to know why you're here, or just as important, why the organization is here? Just as in Significance, where we need to feel important to the world, in Vision we need to know our place in the world. In developing teams I have found it very useful and highly effective to develop a Shared Vision where the entire group has input and adds Value. People feel more like the Shared Vision is a part of them if their ideas are included.

To develop a Shared Vision it is important to take into consideration the values of the individuals involved. So a starting point may be the same question we used to see our own values. "What is most important to this group in this organization?" By asking this question we will be able to determine the values that are shared amongst all of the members of the group. We then can set up the priority by asking the individuals to take their list and see what is most important. Then the facilitator takes all of the lists and writes up the final prioritization. From there the group works together to describe in one to two sentences how this value will manifest itself in the environment. Once this Shared Vision is developed it should be used at all levels in all areas of the company or organization. If a question arises on how to handle a situation, anyone in the organization should be able to turn to the Shared Vision statement and find a solution. How much more effective do you feel an organization will be with this guiding force behind it?

General Norman Schwartzkopf, in leading the Gulf War used a shared vision. Everyone knew, "This is why we are here!" When conflicts came up with members of the coalition he would ask, "How does this help us reach our goal?" At this question, all conflicts disappeared.

### Strategic Thinking / Results Focus

Great! So now we have a strong team and they are working well on problem solving and successfully getting assigned jobs completed. The next level is Strategic Thinking and Results Focus.

What is Strategic Thinking? Strategic Thinking is the ability of a team to plan for contingencies in their operation. What do we do if...? New product development flows freely from Strategic Thinking; new solutions to old problems come from Strategic Thinking. You may be thinking, I don't need to have a true team for us to think strategically. We have people in our organization whose job it is to do that. That might be true, but your team will be much more functional and flexible if they are all thinking along the same lines of strategy.

How do we foster Strategic Thinking? The best way is to ask questions. What?? That's it? Yes, that is it. By asking questions of each other and ourselves we can develop Strategic Thinking. What type of questions could you ask your team to inspire strategic thinking? Here are some suggestions.

1.  What happens if everything works exactly the way that we plan?
2.  What could happen if we planned incorrectly?
3.  What contingencies have we not thought of yet?
4.  What is not being said?
5.  If those are the guidelines, what is outside those lines that we have not thought of yet?

6. Has anyone ever done anything like this? How?
7. Is there someone we could model?
8. If this way does not work, what is another way?
9. If we have multiple ways to get to the goal, is there a way to combine them to get to the goal faster or more efficiently?
10. Do we have the right team? Is there something missing? Do we need another resource to be added?

There are team games that are designed to help foster Strategic Thinking as well. Bringing in a consultant to help facilitate some "out of the box" thinking can be very useful. What may also help is to take your team off site to get a fresh perspective. There are many experiential learning facilities across the country, which cater to organizations that want to develop creative thinking. Of course, if you want you could also hire me. Strategic Thinking and Results Focus go hand in hand. When everyone is focused on the result that needs to be accomplished it allows for freethinking.

Have you ever been involved in an organization that *seems* to work very well, yet everyone is going in different directions? You get to the end of the fiscal year and look at your "goals" and say, "Hey, I did not know we had *that* goal." Show me an organization that has exceptional results and I will show you an organization that is focused on the result. Strategic Planning must revolve around the common results that the organization is moving toward. If not, the plans have no focus and will not be achieved.

Well there we have it, Certainty, Significance, Team/Connection, Values/Shared Vision and Strategic Planning/Results Focus. By implementing this model, you can achieve incredible results in your organization. Within this high-functioning team, remarkable managers will develop and your organization and business will soar. If we look at all the pieces to this puzzle, can we be effective leaders if any one of these components is missing? The answer is, "Yes, we can be effective," and, "No we cannot be as effective as we should be." Even at the top end of Strategic Planning / Results Focus, without the base of Certainty, members of our team will not even be able to share ideas for fear of being wrong. Without the Significance that boosts confidence, members of the team will not share for fear of being seen as not being of value to the team. If members of the team feel no Connection with the rest of the team, they see themselves as outside and are not willing to participate fully. It is readily evident how all of these levels intertwine, yet are dependant on each other. There will be times that you or one of your team does not feel like they are at the same level as the rest of the team. This can be expected and planned for. In those times, you as a leader in a management role will need to recognize which of these levels needs to be supported. Then implement a plan to help that individual or the team to, once again, achieve the massive results that they have come to enjoy and expect under your guidance.

## About
## Chuck Schultz

Chuck Schultz is a Personal Development Life Coach that has been through extensive training with Robbins Research International, an Anthony Robbins company. He is also a member of the International Coach Federation and a participant in the Coach University, Coach Certification program. As a coach, Chuck is known for his enthusiasm and determination to achieve results. He was the Head Coach, Trainer, and is now a Facilitator for Anthony Robbins & Associates, Chicago, were he is responsible for training the Coaching Team, as well as ongoing coaching for participants in Anthony Robbins & Associates, Masters Track program.

As a trainer in Team Dynamics, Chuck has quickly received recognition from his peers as an effective and enthusiastic motivator and leader. He is trained in Team Building, including work on high and low level ropes challenge courses. As a business leader, Chuck owned and operated a nationally known, non-destructive testing company. Within two years of fully taking over this company, Chuck returned it to profitability, and was able to sell the company in December of 1999. After selling his business, Chuck wanted to help others achieve their dreams and goals in life. He began Dragon Dynamics, Inc. in January of 2000 and has never looked back.

Chuck's practice focuses on The Entrepreneur and The Executive. He uses tools and assessments such as DISC and

OAD to look at all sides of a situation. Chuck uses a distinctive business solution model to evaluate the client's role within their business, which can also be used to examine the organization as a whole quickly and effectively. Then all that remains is to implement solutions.

To contact Chuck, call 847-873-0492 or send an email to Chuck@DragonDynamics.com. You can also visit his website at www.DragonDynamics.com

# Tools for the Millennium Manager

## By Claire Walsh

When you were promoted to management, you were probably quite excited, looking forward to the challenge and wanting to make a big difference. You had seen how some managers mistreated their employees and perhaps you were a victim of one of them. Now you want a chance to make things right, to manage your employees the way you would have preferred to have been managed, and to really contribute to your employees' success, as well as your own. So, you've accepted the challenge; you're pumped up, ready to make a difference; and you're anticipating the best from your employees. But despite your enthusiasm and desire to maximize employee contributions and performance, you are struggling with your own issues. Maybe you even struggle with your manager. Either way, this impacts your results.

Let's look at three scenarios from an employee's perspective of what it feels like to be managed by you...

Cindy was exhausted, lying flat out on her bed in her hotel room, barely able to lift her arm to answer the phone that was beckoning her to respond. She hesitated for a moment and then reluctantly picked up the receiver and muttered a weak hello. Although it was 9:47 p.m. and her lights were out long ago, her boss was demanding a recap of the sales meeting with the new client. Her boss needed to know how the meeting went because he was catching a flight early the next morning and Cindy's results would largely impact his next move. After a 40-minute conversation, Cindy ended it abruptly and requested her boss not call her after hours again. Now wide-awake and restless, she dropped the receiver and lay back on her perched pillows contemplating her next move.

This wasn't the first time she had been called well after business hours, it wasn't the first time she had traveled wee hours in the morning to get to the client, and it wasn't the first time that she had back-to-back appointments that would get her home after midnight. When would it end? She loved her job, she loved her customers, she was a great contributor, but she was tired of it all—exhausted, worn down, and burned out. She wondered if things would ever change. The first five years with the company were fabulous, she was climbing the ladder, sales were soaring, excitement and enthusiasm prevailed. The small start-up company was thriving and now acquiring its second buy out. Of course, there were also layoffs because companies have to stay competitive, but she had survived them all. Now she was wondering, was she the lucky one or were the others more fortunate?

~ ~ ~ ~ ~

Sharon was a technical expert in her field and other software engineers looked up to her for her knowledge and expertise. She was so good that her boss wanted her to manage the department upon his promotion to Vice President. As a technical expert, Sharon knew the ins and outs of the business and the product line. Sharon knew everything about how to patch fixes to keep her clients happy. When she was promoted to manager, her colleagues were excited because she was so well respected. But Sharon didn't know the first thing about how to manage. She was technically good, but her people skills were deficient. Her employees suffered, the products suffered, and Sharon herself began to suffer. In over her head, her staff was beginning to lose respect for her and they no longer turned to her or counted on her for advice; they simply ignored her and did their own thing. Morale was down, deadlines missed, customers were screaming for updates, and Sharon was on probation for poor performance. How did a star performer end up like this?

~ ~ ~ ~ ~

"You've got to be kidding! I thought we had six weeks for system implementation. There is no way we can do this in two weeks! When did they decide that and who decided that?" Harvey is in charge of the client management system and working with the vendor to get the new system up and rolling. But this news set him back. Why does it need to be implemented in two weeks, when they had an agreed-upon schedule and were on target for implementation? Why wasn't he involved in the changes and worse yet, why is he hearing this from his peers? Harvey wondered if he was being replaced. Was there something else they weren't telling him? And more importantly, how is he going to make this happen and, if he doesn't, should he be looking for another job?

~ ~ ~ ~ ~

Although these stories are fictitious, how unpleasantly familiar they sound! Good, hardworking employees turned off by insensitive, inconsiderate, and off-handed management. Okay, of course, there is always another side to the story—the manager's perspective.

Managers have their own issues to deal with that largely impact how they manage their employees. Let's look at it from your (the manager's) perspective for another view of the situation.

You're the manager and your boss is pushing hard for third quarter results. You've been working 70-hour weeks, including weekends, and this has been going on for some time with no end in site. You're beginning to resent the extra demands, especially since you've had to take over another department due to cutbacks, and finding a replacement is not in sight. There is no light at the end of the tunnel—there isn't even a glimmer. Your new workload requires more frequent travel, you haven't seen your family in weeks, and your kids are wondering if they will ever take that summer vacation you promised them last year.

The job pays well—the money is great and the benefits are fabulous. You really love your job, if it weren't for the unreasonable demands and expectations and constant last minute changes. Hey wait, doesn't that sound familiar—a bit like the employee's needs? And you have to keep that job, especially since you just bought your dream home. But sometimes you wonder if it's all worth it. Wouldn't it be better to have a less demanding job, maybe less money but more time to enjoy life? But there is no time to really look around for other work or even consider your options.

Again, you're on the road racing to catch your 7 p.m. flight. After you check in well after 9 p.m. you need to call Cindy, your top sales employee, to strategize about her approach for landing a new client. It's well after business hours, but what the heck, you have to get this done. And besides, it's after hours for you as well; certainly she'll understand.

You dial Cindy's number and as you wait for her to pick up the phone, your mind races to the deal you just closed earlier that week.  There's an urgent rush to get the client management system functional within two weeks.  Having it installed was the deciding factor for closing the deal.  You haven't even spoken to Harvey, the supervisor for the department you are now overseeing, who is in charge of implementation. But frankly, he is just going to have to deal with it.  You don't have the time to coddle him and explain why you moved the date up—this client is huge.  Harvey will just have to do whatever it takes to get it done.  You'll call him sometime tomorrow, when you get a minute.

You check your voice messages and learn that one of your largest clients is threatening to take business to a competitor because the system patches are not fixing the problem as guaranteed. Sharon, the newly promoted manager, has lost control of her staff and now she herself is out of control.

Does this sound familiar?

Seeing how well-intentioned managers might get caught up in their challenges and lose sight of their larger role is easy. With budget limitations, staff cutbacks, downsizing, and competitive pressures, managers are being forced to take on more and more work that appears to be indispensable to an efficient running company. Too many demands, time crunches, not enough bandwidth to manage and evolve your staff, and a feeling of overwhelm seems to prevail. And employees and managers are both feeling it. Seeing the story from two sides, it isn't hard to have a little sympathy for the manager as well. But in today's struggling business environment, sympathy isn't valued—it isn't even a blip on the radar screen.

Managing is often described as getting work done effectively through the available human resources. And while that is an important part of what managing is about, I also believe there are other elements that separate "just" managing from "remarkable" managing. Management involves creating an environment for employees to thrive in and inspiring them to live their potential, so they contribute fully to the organization. Remarkable managers want the best for their employees; they recognize and appreciate their contributions and value their input. They want for their employees what they want for themselves—respect and the opportunity to flourish. They invest in their employees for the short and the long term. But some managers are fearful that if they help their employees achieve success, it somehow weakens their value and makes them appear less effective. They couldn't be further from the truth.

In my experience over the past years in human resources, I often observed newly promoted managers wielding their power to gain control of a situation, only to be totally out of control. Managing in the Millennium requires the manager to have strong boundaries and standards, and to get their needs met outside the work environment. Millennium Managers don't tolerate inefficiency and under-performance. They create problem-free zones rather than just solve problems, and they serve as a model for others; it's not enough to be just an expert manager. Managing well in today's environment takes excellent coaching skills, self-management, integrity, and courage. I wonder if the employees in the scenarios above would have experienced better results if the manager possessed even some of these traits.

The question is "How could this manager have kept the situation from deteriorating?" Or, "How could this manager have fostered a work ethic conducive to an atmosphere in which their dedicated employees could thrive?"

Let's explore some of the mistakes the manager made regarding the stories presented at the beginning of this chapter. These mistakes are critical in that they rob the workforce of its precious resources, preventing them from contributing optimally and being a value-added asset to the organization's success.

## Top Mistakes Managers Make and Remedies to Avoid Them

### # 1: Lacks Clear Boundaries

First, let's look at how Cindy's boss might be creating a situation of having a burned out employee. Often, making unreasonable demands and impositions on others is an indication that the manager may not have enough respect for him/herself. And, lack of respect for self invariably results in lack of respect for others. Having unrealistic expectations of others could also suggest that the manager's boundaries are weak. If a manager isn't willing to respect his or her own time constraints, he/she cannot expect others to respect them either. A manager who cannot gracefully say "no" to requests that exceed what is normally considered practical, likely will impose unfair demands on others. Remarkable managers must have clear boundaries that allow them to comfortably operate in a challenging environment without losing sense of self.

Having strong boundaries allows one to say "No" to others when it is appropriate. Being willing to say "enough is enough" takes courage and sets the tone for future requests. Normally, saying "No" can open the door for further communications and understandings that lead to a more productive workforce. The downside is that it can sometimes lead to less desirable results, such as unemployment. This is where courage and integrity come in. Speaking your mind and asking for what you need takes courage, especially if you have something at stake. Honoring what you need and speaking your mind, knowing that it frees up others to do the same, takes integrity. By asserting your truth, clearly enforcing your boundaries, and making strong requests to get what you need, you begin to create a thriving work environment that reflects respect for your staff. Remarkable managers make it safe for employees to take a stand when they believe it respects their boundaries.

### # 2: Fails to Provide Support

Sharon appeared to be a star employee on her way to management. Unfortunately, as is often the case, she was promoted without any real training or preparation for her new role of managing others. Promoting within a company can be a good thing as long as the person is properly prepared for the opportunity. All too often, competent employees are promoted because they are experts in their field and they are doing a superb job. Assuming that they can then transfer that skill/knowledge to management is erroneous. Rarely are they successful if they haven't been primed for managing. Sharon was left with little support to carry out her duties and the consequences cost her a client and possibly her career. Most employees want to succeed, to grow and evolve into their new position, but they need the support to do so.

When choosing an employee for succession, it is critical to look at other indicators of success and not base decisions solely on how they operated in a previous position. While it is generally assumed that a person's previous performance will determine how they will perform in the future, it is not a sure formula for shifting from employee to manager, because the skill sets are different. Another aspect of this mistake is assuming that all employees need the same type of support, and failing to recognize that employees need what is appropriate for their level and expertise and in a way that they can receive it. Just as you wouldn't treat all plants alike by exposing them to the same amount of sun or shade or putting them on the same watering schedule, you can't assume a cookie cutter approach to coaching your employees.

Managers with remarkable skills have the systems, structure, and support in place to help their employees succeed. They have a basic success plan for the new manager regardless of the level of management to help them transition. This plan includes knowledge of the newly promoted person's personality and strengths. It includes making sure they have access to information and are connected with the right people so they have the tools to get acclimated to their new role and become productive as soon as possible. Remarkable managers uplift and catapult their employees to success.

### # 3: Communicates Poorly

As is often the case, a lack of communication from his manager regarding changes to a proposed plan has not only frustrated Harvey, he is also contemplating his job security. Commitments made without assessing the impact on those responsible for carrying out the project can be financially costly, if not a morale buster. Not communicating changes timely and directly with the individuals involved undermines employees' trust in management. The manager recognized he failed to inform Harvey of the change in the implementation schedule, but he didn't really care. And, he probably wasn't aware of the consequences of Harvey's deteriorated attitude. It may not have been the manager's intent to slight Harvey, but the result is that he did.

Managers don't intend to forget to communicate key information, but all too often they do, and the impact on the recipient is demoralizing. As an employee, you can probably remember the experience of being in the dark, the feeling of being left out and not understanding the direction of the company. Perhaps managers told you that you didn't really need to know and they would inform you when you did. Or maybe they said it was confidential and they couldn't share it. Your perception was that they knew more than they were telling you and it wasn't always confidential. You might have concluded that they just didn't want you to know—they didn't trust you.

Not getting employees involved in decisions that will impact their work, or at a minimum, not keeping employees informed, discounts the employee and leads to poor morale. Employees need to know what is going on and, even if it's bad news, they will normally respect management more if they have a heads up. Giving employees an opportunity for input is ideal, but just listening to their concerns will go a long way in showing you understand. Some managers thrive on being "in the know" because they think it gives them more power. It doesn't. It makes them look weak and ineffective. Managers with remarkable skills communicate with their employees and value their opinions so they naturally include them where possible in key decisions. They don't react to their own boss, but communicate and "manage up" to help their boss win.

Let's look at two more scenarios of mistakes managers make from the employee's perspective and techniques to avoid problems in the future.

### # 4: Needs to be Right

After his last experience, Patrick vowed he would finally harness his entrepreneurial skills so he could control his own time and be in charge of all the decisions. But there he was again reporting to the lead technician who wasn't even his supervisor. She had been there a little longer than he had, and their mutual boss allowed her to be in charge. The boss was getting good at dumping responsibilities in the name of "delegating" skills. Patrick dreaded going to work because no matter what he did, it wasn't right according to her. She always had an opinion, she always had the last word, she was critical and attacking, and everything had to be done her way. There was no room for creativity, no room for deviation, no room for another opinion; there wasn't any room for the two of them. What was so annoying was that often she didn't even have the answers, but pretended to know it all. The thought of searching for something better in the depressed economy left Patrick paralyzed. But because of the difficulty with this aspect of his job, he finally did.

Being real and authentic takes courage. If you are willing to risk looking foolish, and admit that you don't know everything, you will gain respect, especially if you can demonstrate that you can find the answers. Some managers have to be the ones with all the answers, the "go to" person who knows everything. And because they don't have the answers, they pretend they do. They tend to criticize and intimidate others to keep the upper hand. They focus on weaknesses and point out errors of their staff. By attacking others, they try to keep the attention off themselves and their own insecurity. Employees can see right through this behavior and resent working for bosses who don't have the courage to allow their employees to see their humanness. In an attempt to gain control, these managers try to control their staff, but they are the ones out of control and it shows. They would rather be right than get results.

Managers of the Millennium with remarkable skills know they don't have to know it all. They do have to know their job, but they will never have all the answers. And they are okay with that; there is nothing to prove. These managers aren't afraid to take off the mask. Instead of pointing out failures and criticizing, they endorse effort and growth.

# #5: Steps Over Problems

Marcie was always involved in everything, even the things that weren't her business. She was always overworked and let everyone know it, but she could never keep her fingers out of everyone else's business. She handled every minute detail, thrived on gossip, spread rumors, and was the first to let others know she had the inside scoop. You recognize this person. She knew a lot and everyone depended on her, so it was easy for her to get away with being a marginal employee. Her numerous managers labeled her a "high-maintenance" employee, taking up everyone's time, producing little. She was passed from manager to manager; each one hoping the next manager would finally deal with her. But despite her ineffectiveness, she kept getting satisfactory performance reviews and marginal salary increases because no one wanted to face her wrath.

There seems to be at least one high-maintenance employee in every organization. And what is truly amazing is that this employee can exert more power than the CEO! Marcie had everyone wrapped around her fingers. Each boss, reluctant to deal with her, hoped the other manager would finally pull the reins in. What prevented these managers from recognizing the early symptoms or clues of potential problems? What would it take to get her off the knowledge/power kick and on to more constructive time management and work results?

Managers of the Millennium communicate it all; they don't step over problems or withhold constructive feedback. They interfere immediately and address negative situations when the subtle clues warn them this employee is headed down the wrong track. They don't make decisions based on fear of legal retaliation; they just do the right thing. And, because they are consistent in their approach, legality normally isn't an issue. They don't tolerate nonsense and they don't allow their employees to play small. They focus on the employees' strengths and empower them to take better and more constructive action. They do this with an edge, yet with a gentle, benevolent approach.

～ ～ ～ ～ ～

We've seen five common mistakes managers make and remedies for success. There are many others not mentioned here. However, by focusing on just these five, you will experience a huge difference in your relations with your staff and in eliciting results that will help the organization thrive and be a win/win for all.

We often hear that employees are our greatest assets, and yet we don't often treat them as such. But that is a thing of the past for the new Millennium Manager. The remarkable manager has strong boundaries and the courage to take action, he/she gently, yet effectively confronts issues, supports and enhances his/her staff, and is willing to take risks. This new manager can effectively direct and lead employees at all levels of development, can uplift them and support them in getting their job done well, and can create an atmosphere that nourishes them while helping them manage their career.

Aristotle believed that courage is the first of human virtues because it makes other virtues possible. If having courage is the underlying theme for managers to aspire to, then just like a muscle, it needs to be exercised to become strong or it will become flaccid if not used. As a Millennium Manager with remarkable management skills you'll have plenty of opportunity to exercise that muscle if you choose to accept the challenge.

My deepest wish for you is that you tap into your wisdom, operate from your own strength, manage from your true self, and step out of your fears and into your greatness. I challenge you as a manager with remarkable skills to be willing to try on a new mask—a real and authentic mask that fits the Manager of the Millennium.

## About
## Claire Walsh

Claire, a native of New Jersey, moved from the Jersey Shore to the Denver metro area in the early 70's and has found the Colorado climate and spectacular scenery quite favorable for her outdoor interests in biking, golfing, and hiking. She is passionate about maintaining a lifestyle that integrates her personal interests with her desire to encourage others to live their purpose and do it effortlessly.

Blending 20 years expertise in Human Resources in both the public and private sector, with an emphasis in high-tech, a Bachelor of Science in Management, and professional coach training through Coach University, Claire inspires individuals to discover their passion and live their potential. She has worked in corporations with employees and managers to remove barriers to understanding and increase productivity and morale.

As a Life Coach, Speaker, and Author, Claire does what she loves and helps others do the same by working with them to gain fulfillment in their personal and professional lives. She works with employees, managers, career seekers, and individuals in personal, business, and life transitions to help them stretch, grow and evolve, and move forward. Claire loves working with individuals to support them in making changes, especially the internal changes necessary to create the life they want. Her clients develop clarity, focus, and direction and discover ways to integrate their values with their work. She believes everyone has within them the personal power to create the kind of life that will bring true joy and happiness. By tapping into the wisdom within, clients reawaken their spirit, step out of their fears and live life more fully.

Claire has demonstrated effectiveness in coaching individuals to achieve greater understanding of themselves, and to make informed decisions for optimal results and greater satisfaction. Her coach training is through Coach University, and she is affiliated with the International Coach Federation and the Denver Coach Federation. She is currently enrolled in the Graduate School of Coaching. Claire is also a contributing author to *A Guide To Getting It: Achieving Abundance.*

To find more information about her coaching services, speaking engagements, or other events, visit www.EffortlessTransitions.com.

You may also call Claire at 303-796-9887 or email her at Claire@EffortlessTransitions.com.

# Lighting the Fire Within

## By Ursula Pottinga

"Lighting the Fire Within" began as a renewal retreat for groups and teams. The presentation of this topic gives me joy, is fun, and I get to work with my dear colleague and friend, Judy. It is also a topic that I feel very strongly about. I believe that each and every one of us are called to contribute to our world with all the gifts and talents we have. I believe we do not serve our families, our communities, and the world at large by "putting in time" at work— when we live waiting for weekends to come, so we finally can enjoy ourselves, happy that the week is over. John Ortberg in his wonderful book *If You Want to Walk on Water, You've Got to Get Out of the Boat* writes: "When you take on a challenge, it builds the core of who you are, even if you don't perform flawlessly."

In this chapter I invite you to take on the challenge of getting out of your own boat, so that you may walk on water.

Shortly before I was approached by Marilyn Schwader to contribute a chapter to this book, I attended a networking event organized by my local chapter of Executive Women International.

The speaker, Andrea Pollari of Randstad North America, which is a subsidiary of the Netherlands-based Randstad Holdings nv, the fourth largest workforce solution provider in the world, shared some valuable information and statistics. In 2001, Randstad North America asked a leading marketing and research firm to conduct quantitative research with over 2,600 members of the full-time and contingent segment of their workforce. The result of this research offers insights on employee satisfaction and motivation. In this comprehensive study, the components of the ideal job were explored, as well as how employees define success in the workplace. The survey also examined the current levels of employee satisfaction against the stated components to determine the degree to which employees' expectations were being met.

The results of the research showed that for employees, jobs and success are about much more than money. Work that gives them personal satisfaction, work that is valued, opportunities to learn new things, and even fun were all essential elements.

I would also like to share a personal experience with you. A couple of months later I attended the International Association of Facilitators conference in Dallas. Here I experienced what is possible when people are passionate about their work, who want to make a difference, and who are fully engaged in the process of learning and growing. And more than that, I found participants questioning the status quo and venturing into the world of intuition, creativity, and faith. Over the course of the three days, I saw a deep need for us to connect and share our humanity and life experience on a deeper level. In my own experience and working with many clients on this challenge, we certainly need strategic plans, performance reviews, and analytical skills, but we short-change ourselves when we ignore or belittle the necessity of including our hearts, our faith, and our intuitive intelligence.

Choosing the topic of "Lighting the Fire Within" for this chapter is no coincidence, as I see a direct link between contributing all of our talents and gifts, and the success of the companies we work for. Working with business owners and entrepreneurs, and through my own experience as a former employee, the components of learning, gaining personal satisfaction in our work, and having our work valued is connected to how much or how little we let our light shine and how much permission we give ourselves to include our hearts and souls, as well as our intellect.

This will be easier to do for some people than for others. This will be easier in certain work "cultures" than in others.

But how much do we lose if we do not try to incorporate all of our senses and capabilities?

As a coach, it is my privilege and responsibility to turn the dimmer switch back up for my clients and to provide a space where they can test their own fire and its impact on the world. As a person, it is my gift and assignment to open the doors and bring into your field of vision the possibility of including what we so often leave out. As a manager, it is your privilege and responsibility to create an environment of trust in which your employees are encouraged to stretch, be creative, learn from mistakes, and show up with all the talents and gifts that they have to offer. How can this be done, you ask?

I have outlined a process with questions and exercises that has come out of my experience working with my clients. It is a step-by-step process that I invite you to take on over time. The process takes commitment and staying power to create sustainable changes in yourself, your employees, and the company culture. I also invite you to be patient with yourself and trust that you can do it!

The process that we will be working with is designed to help you create an environment of trust in which employees can fully contribute with confidence. It is also a process that mainly focuses on you and your insights. It is not a process that is about trying to change others, but rather to make changes within yourself, and then notice the impact these changes have on others. I have included ideas that you can put into place to positively influence your employees. However, you will notice that the main portion of the work is done by you.

By working with and implementing some of these concepts and ideas, you will, in fact, light their fire within. All the steps outlined will support you in creating trust so that your employees will respond with confidence. The questions that are posed are for you to ponder and explore, the exercises are created so that you may take what you have learned and apply it in your workplace. The approach is two-fold: a) you learn by thinking about and answering the questions put before you and b) the exercises will help you put the learning into action.

Steps to *Lighting the Fire Within*:

- One – Geting clear about the culture you want to create
- Two – Being a role model for your employees
- Three – Overcoming your barriers and defenses
- Four – Building trust and influencing others
- Five – Lighting the fire within

## Step One: Getting Clear About the Culture You Want to Create

By observing and working with different organizations—both in the profit and non-profit sector—I have discovered that every company, every organization has it's own culture. I have seen that the values, assumptions, backgrounds, and philosophies of the leaders of these organizations create these cultures. These influences are expressed in the Mission Statement and in the attitude of its employees. When a company culture is created around learning, creativity, feedback, and one's life values, employees are happy. There is also a direct link between happy employees and satisfied customers.

Let me give you an example. My family and I live about 30 miles west of Minneapolis. It is a beautiful, wooded area close to Lake Minnetonka with peaceful views of marshlands and ponds. We have deer grazing in our backyard, bunnies eating tulips, and the occasional garter snake sunning on the warm stones that surround the pool. Needless to say, we sometimes have that wildlife entering the house! To combat that, we have enlisted the help of Plunkett's Pest Control and for years Gerry has come to help. Bee's nests in the pool house or under the bird feeder, a snake in the kitchen, a mouse in the basement? No problem! Gerry will come to the rescue: promptly, cheerfully, efficiently, and with treats in his pockets for the dog. He returns my calls within the hour, shows up when he says he will, and he certainly dropped everything when I reported the snake in the kitchen! I am a satisfied customer who has been dealing with him and his firm for years, not only because of his ability to remove the offending wildlife, but because of his positive attitude and upbeat outlook. I would not want to work with anyone else. What is the culture he works in? How does his attitude contribute to and reflect this work culture?

We all contribute to creating the work culture by our values and attitudes. In this first step, I would like you to think about the culture that you want to create. Use the following questions to get clear on "your ideal work place" and the components that make this possible:

- What are your values?
- What matters to you most?
- How do you express these values?
- Are you honoring your values or not?
- What frustrates you; what gives you joy and fulfillment at work?

### Exercise One: Create Your Ideal Workplace

After answering the questions above, take a look at the wheel on the next page. I have taken from the Randstad Survey some of the most important criteria people want to have in their workplace and created the "Ideal Workplace Wheel." Compare this to your own ideals. What do you want to add or change? What is important in your business?

Draw the following wheel on a piece of paper and rate your sense of satisfaction (as it is now) with each segment (on a scale of 1-10, 10 being the highest).

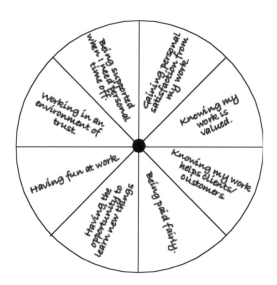

Figure 1: The Ideal Workplace Wheel

Now look at what the wheel looks like. How bumpy would the ride be? See if the low scoring and high scoring areas of the wheel reveal a pattern. Are they related in any way?

Next, choose two low scoring areas that you want to improve and commit to taking action on over the next three months. Ask yourself these questions:

- What are the two areas that you would like to work on?
- What do you want the score to be in three months?
- What will you do to get there?
- What action steps are you willing to take?
- Who will you be accountable to?

Now that you are clearer on the culture you want to create and the impact of your own values and attitudes, your next step in the process of lighting your own and other's fire is to begin the process of creating trust. I believe that only when we feel valued and accepted can we truly shine. Think about a time when that was present in your life. A time when you felt challenged and sure that you could meet that challenge with confidence. I have worked with leaders that inspire this trust, and feel that it is by them modeling certain behaviors that I have been given the opportunity to truly be myself.

What is the example you want to set for your employees? How are you lighting your own fire within? How do you start the process of establishing trust? By becoming a role model.

## Step Two: Being a Role Model to Your Employees

Being a role model to your employees can inspire and motivate them to excel. When working with my clients, I ask these questions:

- Where are you holding back? What talents and gifts are you leaving outside your office door?
- What are your strengths and weaknesses?
- How do you react to feedback?
- What do you know about your employees?
- Who do you want to be as a role model?

By answering these questions, a picture for your own learning will emerge. Out of this learning you can develop a plan. When you discover your points of learning, you can find support and structures to help you expand on your strengths and improve on your weaknesses. What would you need to do to let your light shine brighter?

Think about sharing this experience with your employees. Are you shaking your head now, saying – no way! It is okay to feel uncomfortable about this. Remember, you are beginning a new journey, a path that might not be familiar territory to you. You are opening the box in which you have been for some time, and you may feel vulnerable.

I want to share the story of a good friend, who as a Human Resources Vice President in a large company may have had reason to filter and edit some of her thoughts, ideas, conversations, and emotions. After all, we have much to loose in respect, professionalism, and how we are seen if we reveal too much or (heaven forbid) get emotional or fiery about an issue. However, she is a contradiction of that assumption.

For as long as I have known her, she has fought for what she believed in with an honest, no-holding-back attitude that people have admired, loved, and respected. She has become a role model for many others and me. I see her as a woman whose light shines brightly, who accepts her failures and successes with equal grace, and who makes no apologies for all that she is and still wants to be. She is who she is, and at the same time shows those around her how they can stretch and challenge themselves. She is a perfect example of a role model.

### Exercise Two: Being a Role Model

We have explored your values and attitudes and looked at your strengths and weaknesses. The purpose of this exercise is to take this knowledge and these insights and work on them on a daily basis. As this could become overwhelming, I am inviting you to take this in small steps by concentrating on "one" piece of the puzzle at a time.

Over the next two weeks start each day by deciding:
- Which one gift and talent will I let shine today?
- Which one strength or weakness will I work on today?
- What is one thing I can do today that role models my most important values?

### Step Three: Overcoming Your Barriers and Defenses

So far, we have looked at what culture you want to create and how you can, as a role model, create an environment of trust and value-centered leadership. Hopefully, all this work will translate to you "showing up" more at work and you learning about your comfort zone. In this next step, I want to encourage you to increase this capacity to lead and change. It is possible that you are feeling some discomfort. Maybe people have been commenting on the fact that you are being different. Maybe they are questioning you—maybe they want to know which book you have been reading now!

As you continue on your path:
- What does it feel like for you to be vulnerable?
- What is it like to be seen in a bright light?
- What are you gaining from it? What are the benefits?
- What differences are you noticing in yourself? In others?
- What is the resistance you are noticing?
- Where are you fighting with yourself?
- What defenses are you putting up?

### Exercise Three: Dismantling the Defenses

Visualize the feelings of defensiveness that you are experiencing. What do they look like? Draw a picture of them. Then decide how to break them down. Is it a wall that needs lowering? Are you standing behind it? How much do you want to be seen? What will your organization, your team, or your department get when you step out from behind the wall?

Visualize what it will look like when the defenses are down. Record what you will do.

## Step Four: Building Trust and Influencing Others

After working on yourself, you finally get to venture outside! In step four we are looking to influence others. But before we can do this we must assess and take an honest look at how much trust we have been building in our work environment. When I look at my own life and the life of my clients, I realize that in order to influence others they must first trust. As in the previous step, we are working on creating the right environment for people to thrive in and I believe that trust is the foundation on which to build.

To gain a better understanding of how this might work, I looked at my own life and work and I thought about who and why I trust some people more than others. I observed my interaction with my husband (whom I consider one of the most trustworthy people in my life), my experiences with bosses from my previous life (before I became a coach and all things changed!), and I looked at some of my fellow coaches with whom I collaborate and whom I trust and respect. I started a list of what needs to be present, so that I can trust. The following list emerged.

You inspire trust in me because:

- You don't laugh at my dreams or ideas.
- You listen more than you speak.
- You let me be myself; you treat my vision with gentleness.
- You are honest with me and see me as strong.
- You are visible, alive, and vulnerable yourself.
- You admit when you are wrong.
- You expect more of me.
- You treat me with respect and honor me in front of others.
- You keep our disagreements private.
- You hold yourself to higher standards.

I invite you to build on this list and create your own. Then look at the list and ask yourself: How am I doing here?

Next, we want to get to the place where we can influence others. Now that you have worked on being a role model, living by example, being visible and vulnerable yourself, and looking at trust, you are ready to influence others.

Think about the qualities your employees have and what you would like to see more of. When you interact with your employees next time, ask them questions such as:

- What could we do differently?
- What is your opinion?
- What is important to you?
- What do you think will lead to your success?
- What is one quality you have that we have seen too little of?

Listen to their answers without judgment. Be curious and open to the responses. And notice what you are thinking.

### Exercise Four: The Employee Involvement Challenge

Choose one employee per day that you will engage in this manner. Think about them at the start of the day. What is your intention? At the end of the day write down what was hard and what was easy. How do you feel about the interaction? What is the impact on your relationship with this person?

Remember that this might be a new way for your employees to be, too. Simply be curious about them and keep your own judgment aside. You want to find out more about them and who they are. Ask open-ended questions and listen to the answers. Notice what you are hearing. Also notice what you are seeing.

## Step Five: Lighting the Fire Within

You have been doing great work around your values, living by example, building trust, and influencing others. By now you will see and feel a difference. Maybe the mood is lighter; maybe people are more open, more creative, more outgoing. You will notice the improvements in you and others. You are now ready to light their fire. Notice your energy. I hope you feel excited by the possibilities.

Let's look at both sides of the coin. One side is the safety, holding-back-side. From my experience with working with my clients, I see that when we hold back, when we dim our lights, when we ignore what matters to us, so much is lost to the world. On the other side of the same coin, I have come to appreciate that we are human beings (not human doings!) and it is in our BE-ing that we sparkle, contribute, and find fulfillment. For most of us this is a lofty notion that has a place in our hearts when it comes to our friends, children, and family members. We feel instinctively that this is the very essence of what makes us happy, gives our lives meaning, and enriches the work we do and the lives we touch. When we show up fully, without the filter, life begins to feel easier, joyful, and rich.

In the previous steps, you have worked through and played with a different mindset and a different approach. Now it is time to step it up, to use the foundation of trust that you have built, and encourage others to follow your lead.

- Are you playing a big enough game?
- What are you willing to step up?
- What risks are you willing to take?
- What will you gain by taking these risks?
- What do you need to do, to see and value your employees?

### Exercise Five: Lighting the Fire Within!

You have done a lot of soul searching. You have asked and answered a lot of questions. You have stepped out and stepped up. Now you can apply your insights and use your knowledge to light the fire of others.

For your next group meeting, design an exercise in which all can participate. Ask them to write down the strength that they value most in themselves. Ask them what they would like to contribute more of.

Ask them:

- What is the impact you want to make?
- What is getting in the way?
- What support do you need to accomplish this?
- What are we missing when you hold back?

You might want to make it fun, with different hats to wear or give special awards that honor that quality. Think about what would work in your company and for your team.

As you may have discovered while answering my questions, making the shift from what has been to a different way of thinking and managing is not easy, and it will take time. Be patient with yourself and with others. Any change takes time and will not be without challenges.

If, as a manager, you want to encourage creativity, dialogue, and curiosity, you must create an environment in which people feel unrestricted, seen, and valued.

The benefits to you and your company and the clients you serve are far beyond the efforts and the risks of stepping out of your comfortable box.

In closing, I want to share a memorable experience with you. While facilitating a renewal retreat this year, Judy and I encouraged the participants to share what they value most in life. People were magnificent in their openness, sensitivity, and vulnerability. They were courageous in stepping into unfamiliar territory, which left them connected with each other in completely new ways and opened the door to new possibilities. They truly saw each other that day. And what we saw we honored and respected.

Some people will always be resistant and fearful of that process. Nothing that you will say, provide, and create will coax those people out of the box that they have built to protect and guard themselves. However, as a manager you can continue to provide the environment for those employees who *are* responsive to the changes. Allow your employees to use their creativity, and support them by role-modeling your own brand of faith, intuitiveness, and courage.

I believe God created us to fulfill our purpose. It is our uniqueness that gives our organizations strength and diversity. But this uniqueness has to be fostered and encouraged to grow.

You may know the words of MaryAnne Stevenson:

"Our deepest fear is not that we are inadequate. Our deepest fear is that we are powerful beyond measure."

Believe that you can do this, and you will.

## About
## Ursula Pottinga

Ursula Pottinga, CPCC, is a certified personal and professional coach with an international hotel management background, as well as five years in real estate sales. Her career moved her from Germany, Belgium, England, and Canada to Minneapolis, Minnesota. Her company, Compass Coaching & Consulting, specializes in working with organizations and individuals in time of change and transition.

Her clients include executives who are embracing new jobs, professionals changing careers/industries or preparing for sabbaticals, and business owners and professionals in the hotel industry who are looking for effective structures and strategies that will support them in times of change. She helps her clients connect to their core values and gain a heightened self-awareness of their gifts and talents enabling them to stay focused and motivated, especially in times of upheaval and uncertainty.

She develops and facilitates group work that addresses the development of human potential, managing change, customer service, and money/prosperity issues.

For information about Compass Coaching & Consulting visit her web-site www.CCCcoach.com. You can also call Ursula at 952-449-0409 or email her at Ursula@CCCcoach.com.

# Communicating From Your Heart for Empowered Partnership

### By Margie Summerscales Heiler

How often have you heard that communication—and its resulting level of trust—is the #1 problem in organizations and businesses? Results of employee surveys consistently show that trust and communication are rated as the biggest factors affecting a manager's success. When effective communication and positive relationships are missing in either the manager's business or personal life, he or she feels disempowered. With the resulting energy drain on productivity and people, it's no surprise that communication is so significant to an organization's survival. While poor communication may sound simple to fix at the outset, years of experience and research demonstrate the opposite.

There are many approaches to this perplexing and complex problem. However, what I've found to be one of the most effective things managers can do is hire a coach to help them improve in this critical and vital component to management. Not only have I experienced the positive effects of coaching, I consistently hear from clients and students at the Academy for Coach Training and from managers that coaching changes all relationships in a positive way. The most important reason why working with a coach helps a manager become a better communicator, and thus a remarkable manager, is due to the coaching relationship, a special partnership that is most successful when the client is ready—when communication and trust exist. Because of the magical results in individuals and teams who experience coaching, my dream is that someday coaching will be offered as an employee benefit in organizations. Until then, managers who bring coaching principles to their work will see incredible changes in their organization.

*"Coaching is the sacred space of unconditional love where learning, growth, and transformation naturally occur."*
~ Fran Fisher

The changes I have personally experienced due to coaching have, like a pebble in a pond, had a ripple effect that impacts all my interactions. My learning journey has continued as the lessons of communication and relationship crystallized to a deeper level recently from sources I had not anticipated—my horses and Karen, a gifted horse trainer.

As a youngster, I did the typical pony rides and a few horseback rides and always liked being around horses whenever I had the opportunity. I never imagined then that by my fiftieth birthday I would be living in the country, where I was exposed to horses, the smell of manure, and the urge to own a horse I could ride at any time. After attending the Living Your Vision® class at the Academy for Coach Training, my passion for horses deepened as I began to understand my own essence and purpose in life. I also learned what horses stand for in the animal kingdom—power, adventure, freedom, and spirit. The possibility of owning a horse soon became a reality. Going no farther than a neighbor's mini-ranch, I fell in love with a horse that was just my speed—well-trained, older, and obedient. Her name was Tootsie and she was like Old Faithful. If I had been paying more attention at the time, I would have realized that she was teaching me all the lessons I needed to know about being a better communicator. Much later, I realized that everything I was learning from my horse-owning experience could be applied to employee management. All it took was a little kick in the head...

After my initial beginner horse education from Tootsie, I graduated a few years later to purchasing and contracting my second horse, a ten-year-old mare named Diamond. Notice that I use the word "contract." While I knew about entering into agreements with clients, the thought had not occurred to me that I would have an agreement with a horse. I was told that Diamond was "green broke." You see, horses come in several stages of training. One with minimal training is considered green, meaning that the horse has learned to walk, trot, and canter with a saddle and has been ridden mainly in controlled conditions, such as a riding ring. A skilled rider is needed for the horse to become "finished." What I found was that I was the one who was green broke. When I realized what "green broke" meant, I sent Diamond away for one month of training. In the meantime, I took lessons on another horse that was called a "push button" horse, thinking I would be ready for Diamond when she completed her training. A push button horse is a kind of "finished" horse. It is one that will do most anything you ask and forgive your mistakes. For the most part, thankfully, that was the case. Although I was reaching out to Diamond, I had not learned the horse partnership skills nor experienced them to be in relationship with her.

I had wonderful encounters with Diamond most of the time and am thankful that she turned the other cheek at what I didn't know, for I had always assumed that all I had to do was jump on a horse and ride. I soon realized that the feeling I had of adventure and freedom could be tempered by a couple of traumatic events—including being bucked off a few times. The more I pressured Diamond, the more aloof she became. I wasn't sure what to do, as I was an inexperienced horse manager. Yes, I had learned from many "natural" horse trainers and believed what they said. However, it took personal experience for the lessons to sink in. And this kind of learning flows more easily from a place of partnership and love.

As I've mentioned, the same skills are also necessary for managers. So, let me take you through some of the lessons I learned by becoming a horse owner that helped me become a better communicator, and thus a more remarkable manager—of myself and others.

### Lesson #1: Build a Partnership

Employees want a partnership and a trusting relationship rather than pressure. I find the same is true of horses. Did you ever try to get a horse into a trailer for the first time with pressure instead of partnership? What I see now in retrospect is that I often did not bond with Diamond and she was going through the motions. "Going through the motions" actually inhibits the process of partnership. That type of behavior usually means that something—an obstacle or barrier—is in the way.

Fortunately, at the time I realized that something was not working in my horse partnership, I met Karen, the horse trainer, and consulted with her about my situation. Something was stopping me from having better relationships with my horses. I told Karen that my husband and I had three horses—Diamond, Fancy, and Deuce and described each of them. In the meantime, Diamond had been sick and I had to make a decision about where to focus my energy, as I barely had time to partner with one horse, let alone three. After Diamond's recovery, several lessons with Karen, and a trial with Deuce, we decided that Fancy was the horse for me. She was young, friendly, and eager and also "green broke." I listened and trusted as "good" managers do.

### Lesson #2: Listen to Your Intuition

Listen to your intuition for making decisions. Having true clarity involves your heart and intuitive abilities. I encourage my clients to make their decisions from both their hearts *and* minds after considering options. When managers are stuck in their heads, they do not trust themselves, are disempowered, and the connection between head and heart becomes a barrier instead of a bond.

For me, deciding to partner with Fancy was a huge intuitive leap and commitment as I listened to my heart. Heretofore, I thought I would have a horse and ride her whenever I had the time and felt like it. Simultaneously, something niggled at me about not spending enough time with Diamond. I kept promising myself I would do more and even attended some classes at the local university. I saw a time commitment coming and I wasn't sure I could make that commitment. However, I realized at the outset of the journey that I had to ask my heart, "Do I have the time and am I willing to make the personal commitment to be focused and present in the moment?" Managers must also ask themselves this question. Unfortunately, many don't, making the mistaken assumption that they don't have to pay attention to their employees' needs.

I had noticed something was stopping me from having a better relationship with my horse. To help me decide, I used one of the coaching models from the Academy for Coach Training that I also use with managers and clients: Clarity – Alignment – Action. This particular model demonstrates that being clear about what you want and aligned with that clarity is important before jumping into action. To continue with the horse metaphor, at this point I was clear I wanted to partner with Fancy and jumping into action would not serve either of us well. So, off I went to be coached and learn to ride her. I was aligning with my clarity (planning) before taking action (riding). Since coaching and horseback riding are similar processes, I began "trusting the process" with riding the way I do so naturally in a coaching relationship.

"Surely," I told myself, "the grounding I feel from trusting the process with coaching will translate to my partnership with Karen and Fancy." However, because I was still learning, my head came into the picture. I became a "manager" of my horse instead of a partner in communication. I started running all kinds of tapes through my mind about budget, what it would take, would I be able to do it in the end, etc. These were my "Gremlin" voices getting in the way. To move forward, I continually and consistently went back to my clarity about what I wanted for grounding and asked myself, "What do I want?" What I wanted was to partner with Fancy and have fun. To do this, I had to go inside myself, check out my motives and honor my choices, intentions, and values.

As a manager, what do you want? What are you clear about and how will you align with that clarity for improved business relationships?

During one of our initial sessions, after I decided what I wanted, Karen said to me, "You have to think like a horse." "Okay," I said to myself, "How in the heck do I think like a horse?" First I had to understand how Karen related to horses and how Fancy learned. To do this, I used my knowledge of people and personality inventories to better understand Karen's perceptions, as well as the horse's point of view.

Further, as a manager and coach, I support employees and clients in connecting with their hearts and getting in touch with their innermost feelings. One of the things we find there is love. Decisions from the heart come from a place of love and using intuition. This does not mean excluding mind decisions, for the best decisions are made with both heart and mind included.

## Lesson #3: Never Give Up

Persistence pays off. Love and have patience with yourself on your learning curve as you discover ideas and ways to improve your communication style. Allow mistakes; then get back in the saddle.

"Never! Never! Never! Never give up!"

~ Winston Churchill

In coaching, I often remind clients to be patient with themselves. For my riding lessons, I intentionally made the choice to learn more about the views of both Karen and my horses, in particular Fancy. This took a great deal of patience and truly flexing (temporarily changing) my communication style, as the natural sense of urgency I have that has served me well in many situations was not working in this relationship. I had learned how to flex and taught this to many other managers and employees with tools such as

Insight® Inventory and Myers-Briggs. In this instance, I had gotten by for a while with getting on the horse and riding (taking action) before engaging in clarity and alignment. I chose at this stage to be more on purpose with Clarity – Alignment – Action, instead of giving up.

What I know is that a person's perception *is* their reality; it's how they look at the world. This is also true of horses. Regarding a horse's viewpoint, it doesn't matter if they have no depth perception because the horse is literally looking at the world through a vision you would see if you held a fist up between your eyes. A horse will jump over a little stream or sidewalk crack they think is deep and could swallow them because they have no depth perception. The first time Diamond did that with me on her back, I was quite surprised and held on for dear life. Trusting me enough to take her through the water without jumping took time and baby steps.

For managers, the perception of others about how deep the water is or how large the cracks are is their truth. Their baby steps of trust are supportive of their growth and each one's process looks different. I honor each individual's unique process, as I know it contributes to our synergy and empowers both of us in the relationship. Remember that other people's perceptions are what matters most to them and learning to trust themselves is an evolving, natural part of the process. Employees, including me, are not always sure of their choices, intentions, and values as they test the waters and cracks. This is all part of the learning curve as they move from unconscious incompetence to unconscious competence in "The Competency Model" as described by John Whitmore in *Coaching for Performance*.

During my own learning curve to competency with Fancy, several events made me think my choice was a little suspect. Patience and trust were called for in a big way one Sunday when I became impatient. I didn't honor Fancy's learning curve and decided she needed to become more accustomed to the saddle. I put it on her (without my trusty horse trainer present and without considering the consequences). Well, something tickled her belly and she went into flight mode. She ran and ran around the indoor arena when I let go of the lunge line until she was thoroughly exhausted, had crashed full speed into a metal gate and bent it, and had the saddle hanging below her belly. She was out of control and I was terrified. You can probably imagine how close I was to giving up. As a manager, have you ever felt like giving up? I certainly have—as a manager, and with my horses. For some reason, I persisted. After all, I said, "This requires many of the same skills I use in coaching." Everyone has a process and personal learning curve. I tapped into mine, and realized that Fancy needed to have her learning curve, too, on her journey from "green" to "finished."

At the same time, my dear Gremlin was telling me that I wasn't meant to ride at my age and who in the heck did I think I was. Well, I told my Gremlin how I fondly remembered the way I loved riding up in the mountains with my friend Sue. My Gremlin crept closer and said, "Are you cut out for the patience that horse training takes?" After wrestling with this for a couple of weeks and going through the motions with lessons, I decided that I was up for it and I wanted to think and perceive like a horse. Referring back once again to the Clarity – Alignment – Action model, I had clarity. In coaching terminology, what I was experiencing is referred to as "breakdown." This means the ride is not always smooth. Things weren't working the way they were supposed to. I had to abandon my preconceived notions about my ability with horses and start over with a clean slate as I swallowed my pride. The beauty is there was nothing wrong with that. In fact, having a "breakdown" moved me forward.

I saw how much patience would be required if I were to venture onward. This meant I made a conscious choice about flexing—temporarily changing my natural style to being more steady and patient. This has been an incredibly rewarding and gratifying breakthrough. I am also getting better at doing this in other areas of my life. When we learn something in one area of life, we can apply that success and learning to another area. The good news is that this can happen for you and your employees, too.

### Lesson #4: Communicate with Trust and Respect

As manager and coach, I deeply respect my co-workers and clients. I see that Karen, my horse coach, always respects horses and riders alike. I appreciate that and I wouldn't be riding Fancy today if it weren't for Karen's skill, expertise, keen awareness of surroundings, and ability to listen on all levels simultaneously. Needless to say, bonding with a horse makes a tremendous, life-saving difference since a horse can be dangerous if you are not listening on all levels, profoundly aware, and in communication. This is also true for managers. Karen taught me that Fancy shouldn't be afraid of me—that she should respect me. Imagine a workplace where mutual respect exists and everyone chooses to go to work instead of workers being fearful about their job security.

What if your life was full of trust and respect? When employees and managers enter into a partnership of trust and respect, sacred space as described in Fran's definition of coaching is created. That sacred space is violated when negative experiences affect a partnership. For every bad experience that deepens a lack of trust, it takes time to rebuild security, predictability, and consistency. In everyday life, when someone you are in relationship with experiences negativity or disrespect, they remember it. Trust can be broken down in the snap of a finger and it takes a long time to get it back—if ever. When a manager focuses on trust, that manager attracts trust back. Where is trust present in your life—and where is it missing?

This reminds me of one of the first times I tried to bridle Deuce as a young horse. Of course, he was fearful of this strange object coming at him and I was bound and determined to get it on him no matter what. I had not taken the time to develop trust with him, as I didn't know any better. Wow—was I ever surprised when I got my first kick from a horse. I have a feeling that employees often feel "bridled" by their managers before they have had an opportunity to see and sniff what is coming at them and this creates a lot of fear. Managers want employees to respect them—not be afraid of them.

Being consistent and trustworthy means no more double messages. For example, as part of my training, Karen asked me to trot on Fancy. I gave her the signal and she did what she was supposed to do much to my surprise and delight. Well, I got a little panicked and reacted instead of trusting her. Guess what happened as I pulled in on the reins? She became confused and distracted. This took energy and connection away from the partnership. Fortunately, I acted quickly and consistently to rebuild the relationship. In relationships, when mistakes and miscommunication are overlooked and let go, they become unmanageable. Fancy would have become unmanageable if I had not stepped in to let her know I made a mistake and was clear about what I wanted in our partnership—a synergistic relationship. How often as a manager are you willing to admit you made a mistake? Do you have a place right now in your life where you are afraid to admit a mistake or you feel disrespected?

## Lesson #5: Actively Engage in Your Partnerships and Relationships

Always lead from your heart and your head. This shows that you care, strengthens the bond of partnership, and creates safety.

Sue, a dear friend and client who I ride with, told me that she speaks to her horse through her heart and that when she is riding, she is in her heart, as well as her head. She is an experienced manager and expert rider. As she said this, I knew she was also describing how managers and employees do their best work: when they are truly in touch with their hearts and know their own personal values. We all do better when we are connected with our inner selves. When that connection doesn't exist, horses and employees can sense it, and will immediately react to that missing link.

Most of the time, I am Fancy's leader and she trusts me. I want to understand her. If you are a manager worthy of trust and respect, anyone you are in relationship with will trust you 100%. A good manager is a natural coach, in addition to being a leader. And when you are partnering with a coach, your management coaching skills will spontaneously improve.

If a rider is not engaged with and leading his or her horse, the horse is left to their own devices and he or she will follow the lead mare or herd. Here's an account of what can happen on your ride. The horse will follow or compete or show off with the other horses. For instance, I was delighted when I rode with Sue and Diamond followed her horse. I didn't have to do anything except ride. This meant my horse would do whatever her horse chose to do and had no guidance from me. This left me in some dangerous situations without partnership from my horse. There was no sacred space where learning, growth, and transformation naturally occur. I was not actively engaged, because I thought my only job was to stay in the saddle on the horse, ride, and have fun under all circumstances. In a successful management relationship, everyone is actively enrolled and engaged to co-create the space for learning, growth, and transformation to naturally occur.

Managers and leaders who care about actively engaging in relationships put their principles before their personal gain and they support others—mistakes and all. My clients and co-workers are leaders and we are willing to learn from mistakes and motivate others from our hearts. We model leadership and attract that in others. In healthy relationships such as these, there is no fixing going on. Coaches and remarkable managers believe that everyone is whole and capable and that people want to be treated with respect and dignity. That takes heart, soul, spirit, and partnership. Personally, I know what it's like to lose those as a manager— and with horses—and don't want to learn those lessons the same way again. It took a while for my butt to heal when I was bucked off and a longer time for my organizational wounds to heal when I sold my soul. Now that I'm a coach and have a coach, those situations will not repeat themselves and I won't succumb to that kind of victimhood. Instead, I will respond from an empowered place of partnership and communication. I am committed to heart-centered relationships where partnership happens—with people and horses!

> "REAL COMMUNICATION HAPPENS WHEN PEOPLE FEEL SAFE...
> REAL COMMUNICATION IS A PRODUCT OF TRUST."
> ~ KEN BLANCHARD

In partnerships, managers come to coaches for safety just as people always have naturally gone to their leaders to seek reassurance. In this kind of relationship, managers thrive, as they are comfortable enough to be authentic, step into their greatness, and shine. When managers and their employees feel safe, they give back in all relationships, generate energetic partnerships, and radiate positive energy. Without safety, the ride is dangerous and employees will shut down and do only what they absolutely have to do to get by. This takes a tremendous amount of energy and stifles creativity. Creativity and its expression come from the heart. When people feel afraid and unsafe, they come from their heads with panic and fear. Because they jump into a reactive mode, creativity and energy shut down. People literally close their hearts to protect themselves and sometimes lose their minds, too. I have experienced this in many organizations I have worked in and with as a consultant. My desire is to help other managers on their journeys so they can also have the experience of being empowered and energized. Like

Fancy running endlessly around the arena when she was in flight mode, a lot of wasted energy occurs when employees feel unsafe and are fearful. Pure survival comes first, zapping energy and creativity.

On the other hand, when people feel safe, they accomplish much more and have immediate access to heart, head or mind, and spirit. They feel better, healthier, and more balanced. When energized and engaged, both horses and employees work harder, have more fun, and get more accomplished.

If you have any problems or unmet desires in your relationships and partnerships, how do you and others around you feel? When managers are unsafe to be around, it affects their integrity. Part of a coach's job is to help you learn more about yourself so you can better understand how you feel, how others perceive you, and the impact you are having.

### Lesson #6: Establish Goals to Eliminate Confusion

Karen taught me to have a goal every time I ride. And, if I don't have one, she gives me one! Without a goal, horses will become confused. Without goals and clear objectives, employees will be confused. This reinforces and demonstrates once again the Clarity – Alignment – Action principle of coaching to which I have been referring. Coaching clients and managers hire me to help them reach their goals and highest aspirations as they enjoy the process. They and Fancy look to me for strength and grounding to gain clarity and alignment on their goals. Aligning with them means "doing your homework," that is, similar to the planning and gathering of resources as in Ready – Aim – Fire. Without clarity and a sense of direction, managers don't know where they are headed and neither do their employees. Have you ever jumped into action without a goal—fired without aiming? What happened?

I am clear about my goals when I am riding Fancy on any particular day. We align with the goal before we take action. The journey we take becomes the process. For your goals within the context of Clarity – Alignment – Action, consider Ready – Set – Go or Ready – Aim – Fire. This is a welcome change from when I previously jumped on the horse and took action before being clear and aligning with that clarity. I am having so much more fun now and it's a much safer journey!

### Lesson #7: You are Responsible for Your Results

Much to my dismay, Karen told me early on that she could ride Fancy and train her so she could ride her, but that wouldn't do me any good. At first, I didn't understand this. After all, what difference did it make to the horse who was riding? I soon learned that the horse knows. Getting up on this big, fast horse and learning right along with her took courage, and a willingness to learn—a "beginner's mind." A manager is far more successful with the curiosity of a beginner's mind. Managers who think they "know it all" are far less successful. With Fancy, I am continuously looking for signals about what she is communicating, especially when I'm training her. One thing I've realized is to enjoy her play instead of reacting with fear. This is also what happens in a management relationship. After co-creating a partnership, employees will be willing to explore their fears and enjoy the play and process with amazing results. The manager is responsible for the space created and for the results. Employees will be responsible when you hold a big space for them and support them by being aware of and having empathy with their process.

A good manager doesn't ask employees to achieve goals that are unattainable. Karen has never asked me to do anything beyond my capability that is harmful. While Karen stretches me, she holds my agenda as a masterful coach does and helps me expand—one lesson at a time. She has helped me become a better rider, coach, manager, and person. One of my goals is to help managers make a difference in their lives and, therefore, the lives of everyone they come into contact with—individuals, teams, and organizations—because I believe that everyone comes to the universe with unique gifts and talents to offer and will contribute positively when those are tapped. Uncovering these gifts and talents is what employees of the best managers experience. A manager's—as well as coach's—job is to bring out people's magnificence.

As a manager, are you ready for a coach? I encourage you to write some lessons you want to focus on for partnership from your heart and share them with a coach. Becoming a remarkable manager is hard to do alone. With my coaches, I have learned to enjoy ease and flow in partnerships and relationships. For instance, when I am riding, I continually want to recall immediately all the things I'm supposed to remember that Karen taught me, and that isn't possible. I appreciate the reminders she gives me. Over time, it will come naturally and I'll be ready for the next lesson. My intention is to relax and have fun and I will continue to check in on my lessons from time to time to see what is missing and where I am doing well. My coaches help me do this.

If your employees are not communicating with you, look in the mirror. Your communication skills can make or break the management relationship. A manager without good communication skills is "green," and may get by for the short term. A manager with effective communication skills is like a finished horse, polished and smooth.

Are you willing to learn and grow, to work on building a trusting and respectful partnership with your employees, to listen to your intuition, to get back on the horse when you make a mistake, to establish goals, to be responsible for your results, and to be actively engaged in your relationships? I recommend you enter a coaching relationship so you don't have to embark on your magnificent journey alone. You can begin with your relationship with yourself. As you deepen that relationship, you will find it easier to communicate from *your* heart for empowered partnership. And once you have discovered how to flow and be in that space, you too will become a Remarkable Manager!

"MAKE THE RIGHT RESPONSE EASIER FOR YOUR HORSE TO DELIVER,
AND THE WRONG RESPONSE HARDER TO ACCOMPLISH."
~ FRAN DEVEREUX SMITH

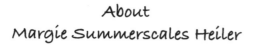

## About
## Margie Summerscales Heiler

Margie is currently Director of and a Senior Course Leader for the Academy for Coach Training in Bellevue, Washington. She also enjoys a successful coaching business from her home in Utah as a Personal and Executive Coach. Margie's experience includes management positions in the corporate world as well as extensive knowledge in business, operations, and the training and organization development fields. Providing coaching for leaders, teams, and businesses, she offers a varied background, along with the following certifications: Myers-Briggs, BenchMarks 360 (Center for Creative Leadership), Selling with Insight, and other models and inventories for improved communication, performance management, exploring personality differences, and strategic planning and growth.

Since moving to Utah, Margie has interfaced with a number of businesses with their training and performance management efforts. She has been on Fox TV, and is also a contributing author to *A Guide to Getting It: Self-Esteem*. Her chapter, "Self-Esteem from the Inside Out," describes the tremendous and magical positive differences coaching has made in her own life, as well as the lives of her clients and students at the Academy. Her clients come from a wide variety of backgrounds, and she serves as a mentor for other coaches.

With her passion and interest in helping people achieve their personal and professional dreams, Margie is truly a visionary leader and champion for growth. Her clients enjoy the partnership, truth, safety, trust, challenge, and fun they co-create with her in the coaching relationship to improve themselves personally and professionally.

Born in Canada, Margie has lived in California, North Carolina, Pennsylvania, Georgia, and Florida and has raised four children. Today, she is creating her life from the inside out and supports others in discovering and living their dreams. She provides guidance for individuals, teams, and organizations to liberate their power as they imagine, plan, and manifest their highest visions. As a result, her clients create intentions and make choices leading to increased self-esteem, happiness, and improved performance and productivity.

In addition to being quoted in an article concerning career changes for *InfoWorld*, she has been interviewed numerous times about coaching and the techniques she uses. Most recently, she was interviewed for a column in a wellness magazine. As a customer service expert, she was honored to assist in the 2002 launch of Smile!, a state-of-the-art video presentation. Giving presentations to a number of societies and groups contributes to her balance and fulfillment as a commitment to professional and community organizations. Currently, she is the Academy representative for ACTO (Associating of Coach Training Organizations) and a member of the ICF Credentialing Committee.

Margie also enjoys family and friends, her pets and horses, music, skiing, dancing, and hiking.

To contact Margie, call (801) 446-0794, send an email to CoachMargie@earthlink.net. You can also find out more about Margie by visiting www.CoachTraining.com.

# Quick Order Form

**Price:** $14.95 U.S., $19.95 Canadian/International

- Fax orders: 801-838-1671. Send this form.
- Email orders: Marilyn@ClarityofVision.com
- Postal orders: Clarity of Vision Publishing
  3529 NE Simpson St., Portland, Oregon 97211.
  Telephone: 503-460-0014.

**Shipping by air:**
U.S.: $4.95 for first book and $3.00 for each additional book.
International: $10.00 for first book; $5.00 for each
additional product (estimate).

**Payment:**
    Cheque
    Credit Card: Visa or Mastercard

    Card
Number:_____Exp. _____

Name on card: _____

For more information about this book or any other of the
books in the *A Guide to Getting It* series, or to order online,
visit:

    www.AGuideToGettingIt.com

For more information about Clarity of Vision Publishing, visit:

    www.ClarityofVision.com